TABLET PC

Quick Reference

Jeff Van West

PUBLISHED BY
Microsoft Press
A Division of Microsoft Corporation
One Microsoft Way
Redmond, Washington 98052-6399

Library of Congress Cataloging-in-Publication Data
Van West, Jeff.
    Tablet PC Quick Reference / Jeff Van West.
        p. cm.
    Includes index.
    ISBN 0-7356-1863-1
    1. Pen-based computers.   I. Title.

    QA76.89 .V36 2002
    004.165--dc21   2002033708

Printed and bound in the United States of America.

2 3 4 5 6 7 8 9   QWT   8 7 6 5 4 3

Distributed in Canada by H.B. Fenn and Company Ltd.

A CIP catalogue record for this book is available from the British Library.

Microsoft Press books are available through booksellers and distributors worldwide. For further information about international editions, contact your local Microsoft Corporation office or contact Microsoft Press International directly at fax (425) 936-7329. Visit our Web site at www.microsoft.com/mspress. Send comments to *mspinput@microsoft.com*.

ActiveX, ClearType, FrontPage, Microsoft, Microsoft Press, Outlook, PowerPoint, Visio, Windows, and Windows NT are either registered trademarks or trademarks of Microsoft Corporation in the United States and/or other countries. Other product and company names mentioned herein may be the trademarks of their respective owners.

The example companies, organizations, products, domain names, e-mail addresses, logos, people, places, and events depicted herein are fictitious. No association with any real company, organization, product, domain name, e-mail address, logo, person, place, or event is intended or should be inferred.

Acquisitions Editor: Alex Blanton
Project Editor: Sandra Haynes
Technical Editor: Robert Lyon

Body Part No. X09-16611

To Mr. C and Baby B.

Acknowledgments

This book would not have been possible without the assistance of many people. On the Tablet PC team, I am especially thankful to Jim Cox and Joanne Burtch for helping get this project rolling by organizing meetings and getting the tools into my hands. Shena Ferree also has my appreciation for getting my tablet updated with the latest software builds. Thanks to Eric Fox, Koji Kato, Anoo Padte, Jeff Pettiross, Cynthia Tee, Kamish Tumsi, and Michael Williams. Each took time to meet with me, share the details of his or her piece of Windows XP Tablet PC Edition, and then answer my barrage of follow-up questions over e-mail. Jeff, Michael, and Suzanne Sowinska also provided valuable commentary on the first draft of this book. Additional help also came from Darrin Fish, Adrian Garside, Kristoff Johnson, Gerhard Schobbe, Darrin Smith, Ravi Soin, and Sterling Tucker.

At Microsoft Press, I am indebted to Alex Blanton for his heroic efforts in making this project happen and to Sandra Haynes for keeping everything running smoothly and handling my questions and odd schedule with good cheer. I am grateful for the work of my editors Robert Lyon and Patricia Masserman for their work in editing this book. My thanks as well to John Pierce for writing the networking section of Chapter 7, to Jennifer Brown for her crucial assistance with my contract requests, and to Brian Johnson for helping me get past the tablet password the first weekend I had the machine so that I could see what the excitement was all about.

Finally, I am thankful beyond measure to Jenny and Charlie Van West for their patience with the stress and long work hours needed to meet the deadlines and make this book a reality.

Table of Contents

Introduction

Why Use a Tablet PC?

"I don't even know where my laptop is [anymore]. I think I lent it to someone."
– Erik Fox, Tablet PC Team when asked if he regularly used his tablet.

Before the Tablet PC ever entered the market, much was written lauding and lambasting the technology, often in the same review. On the positive side, the reviewer would point out the extreme portability, the simplicity of pen interface, and the great potential in using your handwriting for data entry. Almost invariably, the same reviewer would then focus on the errors in handwriting recognition and the limitations of a pen versus a keyboard. While the technology was undoubtedly cool, most people seemed to view it as a novelty worth a few extra dollars on the price of a laptop, but not much more. These reviewers experienced the power of the pen, but then simply missed the point. Yes, the new features are cool technology, but the novelty wears off pretty quickly. What remains is a fundamental change in the way you use, and even think about, your computer. It doesn't happen right away, and I think that's why so many reviewers didn't experience it, but over time it does happen.

Imagine you bought a new car. This car does everything you expect a car to do: drive around town, cruise quickly on the highway, keep you cool in the summer and warm in the winter, play your favorite CDs, and so on. This car has a special feature, however, where at the flip of a switch it turns into a small one-person electric scooter, small enough to pick up and carry with you. All the big car features are still there, you can still drive slow or at highway speeds, have cool or warm air blown toward you, and play your favorite CDs, but the scooter can also carry you slowly along sidewalks, through airports, around the park, and dozens of other places you could never take a car. At first the "scooter mode" of your new car would be a cool novelty, and you might brag about how easy it is to find parking, but you would still use it in car mode for most of your errands and getting around. Over time though, you might use it in scooter mode in ways you never used a car, such as listening to music in a coffee shop or running the heater to keep warm in line at the movies. You might also start using it in scooter mode where you used to use a car, such as running out to the store for ice cream on a clear summer night. Eventually it would change the way you thought about, and even what you expected, from a personal vehicle.

After living and working with a tablet for some time now, I know the device has this perspective-changing potential. The key is that the tablet is a fully-functional computer that can work through a full-size monitor and keyboard and it is a fully-functional computer that can work with a pen and be as unobtrusive as a spiral notebook. You get to keep all the computer functionality you already know, and you get new tools broadening the ways in which you can interact with the computer and use it effectively. Will you now use the pen instead of a keyboard for writing quarterly reports or creating complex spreadsheets? Probably not, but you wouldn't use an electric scooter to drive on the highway either. That's the point of the tablet: you can choose how you want to work from a wide range of possibilities. The point of this book is to help you understand the ins and outs of Microsoft Windows XP Tablet PC Edition and to show you how to use each tablet tool, in the best way, for a given job.

This Book Could Be for You...

This book is written for the person who wants to get the most out of his or her tablet and Windows XP Tablet PC Edition without having to learn it all through trial and error. Because the tablet offers new software, new hardware, and a new paradigm for how you use a portable computer, this book contains a mix of instructions on common tasks, handy tips, suggestions for using pen and speech input, ideas for new approaches to familiar tasks, and anecdotes illustrating how a tablet can change the way people use their computers. It is assumed you are basically familiar with Windows XP and Office XP but don't claim to be an expert. If you are totally new to Windows XP as well as your tablet see Appendix C, "If You're New to Windows XP." The book is designed to complement the tutorial and Help files that come on your tablet, as well as *Microsoft Windows XP Inside Out,* available from Microsoft Press. Where appropriate, cross-references will appear to both these sources.

This book is also for the person interested in reexamining the way they use a computer on a daily basis. I have lived and worked with a tablet for a few months now, taking it across the country and back, using it in meetings, for presentations, and for personal work. In fact, much of this book was written on a tablet. I have also used it to display maps while flying small airplanes and to let my one-year-old doodle without getting ink on his clothes (while I held the tablet of course). As you read, I encourage you to think outside the box when you think about where your computer goes and what it does. I'll provide examples from my experience and those of the Tablet PC team at Microsoft, who have been using their own tablets throughout the software development process.

System Requirements

This book will focus almost exclusively on Windows XP Tablet PC Edition and the Office XP Pack for Tablet PC. To perform most of the actions described in this book, you need only a tablet with Windows XP Tablet PC Edition installed. There are several versions of tablet hardware; the exact model should not matter.

What Defines a Tablet PC

Your tablet is the result of a partnership between Microsoft and several hardware vendors. Microsoft developed the software, and each vendor created their own kind of tablet to meet a specific market need. There are five hardware requirements, however, for any machine to run Windows XP Tablet PC Edition. Here's what they are and what they mean for you:

- **Electro-magnetic digitizer** This system senses the pen position without the pen making contact with the screen and is very accurate. The result is that you can rest your hand on the screen as you work, and the tablet can track your motions much more accurately. There is a sensor for pen-to-screen contact as well, and by combining the two inputs you are able to fully replicate mouse commands with the pen.

- **Rotating video driver that does not require a reboot** You can switch your tablet from landscape to portrait on the fly. This is critical with one-on-one presentation work in which some items you are showing are short and wide and others are long and tall. For tablets with keyboards, this also lets you quickly switch between keyboard and pen input as needed.

- **Resume from suspend in under 2 seconds** Suspend is a short-term sleep mode to extend battery life. If you're running on battery power, you want your tablet to suspend after a short while to save energy, but you want it ready immediately upon waking. It's no good to have the tablet there to jot down a note if you must wait 30 seconds before you can write.

- **Automatically go from suspend to hibernate when the batteries are 75% depleted**   This safety feature protects your work in case you thought the tablet was turned off, but it was actually on standby and the batteries ran out. When the tablet is plugged back in, it can pick up right where it left off with all your work intact, even if you hadn't saved it.

- **No legacy ports**   No tablet will have serial or parallel ports. If you have peripherals requiring these ports, you will need a USB adapter or new USB peripherals.

> **Glossary**   *USB* stands for Universal Serial Bus and allows you to connect and disconnect up to 127 different peripherals to one computer without having to turn off the computer. You often must stop the device before you unplug it.

What Defines Windows XP Tablet PC Edition

Windows XP Tablet PC Edition is a complete version of Windows XP Professional with additional features specific to the tablet. These additional features allow for pen input and control, handwriting and speech recognition, and tablet-specific software. The result is that you can run any program made for Windows XP on your tablet, provided you meet the system requirements for that software. This is similar to how Windows XP Professional is a complete version of Windows XP Home Edition with additional features needed for business users. The differences between these three systems are outlined in Figure I-1.

> **Glossary**   *API* stands for application programming interface and is the code a software developer uses to control the program. The pen, handwriting, and speech APIs allow pen and voice input to applications running on your tablet.

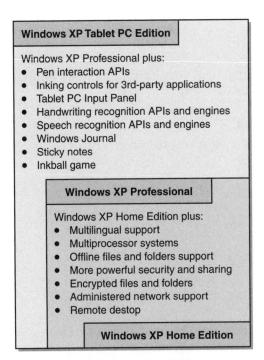

Figure I-1   The features of Windows XP Home Edition, Professional, and Tablet PC Edition compared.

Different Levels of Pen Support

One thing you will find as you use different programs on your tablet is that they support pen input at different levels. This is determined by how the software does or does not incorporate the tablet APIs. Don't worry—all programs that run on Windows XP, even those created before the tablet existed, will allow you to use the pen in place of a mouse and input text using the Tablet PC Input Panel described in Chapter 2. In addition, some software will provide areas for you to enter handwritten information directly into documents as images and control the program through pen movements called gestures. At the highest level of integration, some programs allow you to store the original pen inputs as well as reformat and edit them. Some of these programs come already installed with Windows XP Tablet PC Edition. Others are in development. The possibilities are thrilling.

Support

Every effort has been made to ensure the accuracy of this book. Microsoft Press provides corrections and additional content for its books through the World Wide Web at

http://www.microsoft.com/mspress/support/

If you have problems, comments, or ideas regarding this book, please send them to Microsoft Press.

Send e-mail to

mspinput@microsoft.com

Or send postal mail to

Microsoft Press
Attn: Tablet PC Quick Reference Editor
One Microsoft Way
Redmond, WA 98052-6399

Please note that support for Windows XP Tablet PC Edition is not offered through the above addresses.

Part I

Tablet Essentials

Perhaps more than any other computer, tablets are very personalized machines.

1

Getting to Know Your New Tablet

If you're like me, when you get a new electronic gadget, you open it up and start using it right away, casting aside any instructions or tutorials until something doesn't seem to work or is too convoluted to figure out after an hour of tinkering. I recommend you put off this urge for just a few minutes with your new tablet. The built-in tutorials provide some practice with the pen that will greatly improve your first impressions of your new machine. Once you have some fundamentals down, you can experiment to your heart's content. There are also quite a few customizations you might try that can make your tablet easier to use.

So What About This Pen?

There are really two things to learn about the tablet pen. The first is what you can and cannot do with it and the second is how you actually use it. There are basically five things you can do with the pen and different situations in which you can do them.

- **Use your pen instead of a mouse**   The pen can be used instead of a mouse at any time in any application in which you could use a regular mouse. The pen can provide both left and right mouse button actions.

- **Use your pen in lieu of a keyboard as a text input device**   The pen can be used to input text at any time in any application in which you could use a regular keyboard. The pen accomplishes this using Tablet PC Input Panel.

- **Create ink that becomes a static image** Some applications accept pen inputs and convert them into images. The images can be inserted into documents or attached to e-mail messages.

- **Create ink that becomes both a static image and converted text** Some applications can contain the image of the ink you created and the text recognized from the handwriting. For example, Microsoft Word 2002 with the Microsoft Office XP Pack for Tablet PC allows you to insert your handwriting into a document and shows you the results of converting the handwriting to text.

- **Create rich ink** Currently, only a few applications have this highest level of pen integration, but many more are in development. In this case, you can edit, format, and even search the ink you created.

> **Glossary** *Ink* is a term for the pen strokes you create on the tablet screen. These strokes are not recorded as images. Instead, they're represented by equations describing the relative sizes, angles, and directions of the lines. In different situations, your ink might be converted to text, converted to an image, or saved in its original format.

Tablet Security Button

Microsoft Windows XP is built on the Microsoft Windows NT/2000 architecture, in which anyone using the computer logs in as a specific user. If your tablet doesn't require you to log in using a name and a password, it is actually logging in automatically to a default user account. Depending on whether your tablet was configured for you by a network administrator or you just brought it home from the store, you might need to log on to the tablet using the Ctrl+Alt+Delete key combination. If your tablet does not have a standard keyboard, this can be a bit difficult! The solution is the tablet security button, one of your tablet's hardware buttons, which functions as the Ctrl+Alt+Delete key combination. To see which button is the security button on your tablet, consult the owner's manual that came with your tablet. The hardware button can be used any time you would normally use Ctrl+Alt+Delete, such as when ending a non-responding program, locking your computer while you are away, logging out, or shutting down. All tablets have a security button.

> **Glossary**   *Hardware buttons* are user-definable buttons that are available when no keyboard is connected or the keyboard is hidden. For more information on hardware buttons see "Controlling Tablet and Pen Settings."

Using the Tablet Tutorials

When you power up your new tablet for the first time, you'll see the Welcome To Tablet Computing tutorial, shown in Figure 1-1, designed to give you the basics of using your tablet's unique features. Take a few minutes to go through at least the first six screens, which give you practice using the pen in place of a mouse. Without this practice, your first hour with your tablet will be very frustrating. After the practice section, the next seven screens give you an overview of inputting text using the pen, but there are no opportunities to practice and subsequent tutorials do a much more thorough job on this anyway. Skim through them if you wish, and quit the program. We will cover using the pen to input text in depth in Chapter 2. The most important thing to practice now is using your pen in place of a mouse, particularly pointing the cursor, single-tapping, double-tapping, and right-tapping.

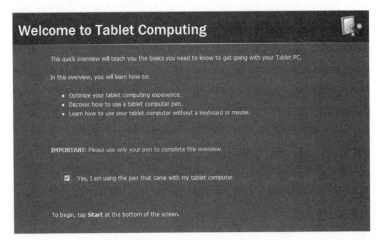

Figure 1-1   Use the welcome tutorial to practice using your pen in place of a mouse.

> **Glossary**   To *tap* is the pen equivalent of a click. Where you would click with a mouse button, you tap with your pen.

Switching the Screen Orientation

The Welcome To Tablet Computing tutorial should be done with your screen in portrait orientation (longer than it is wide) and with the pen as primary input. If your tablet does not have an attached keyboard, it should start up this way. If your tablet can also function as a laptop, it will probably start in landscape screen orientation and with the keyboard and touch pad accessible for input.

The exact process to stow or remove your keyboard and otherwise reconfigure your tablet varies, so you'll need to check your owner's manual. Switching the screen orientation is part of Windows XP Tablet PC Edition and can be done three different ways. Switching the screen is something you might do several times during the day, so you should understand all three.

■ **Use the Tablet And Pen Settings control panel**   Finding a control panel in Windows XP can be a little confusing until you learn what category the control you are looking for fits into. Tap the Start button and tap Control Panel. Tap the Printers And Other Hardware category, and then tap Tablet And Pen Settings. Tap the Display tab and select the orientation you want as shown in Figure 1-2. Because a tablet can be used with any side of the screen as the bottom, there are four possibilities for screen orientation: primary portrait, secondary portrait, primary landscape, and secondary landscape. The labels primary and secondary are arbitrary. Secondary landscape is simply primary landscape rotated 180 degrees. If you switched from primary landscape to secondary landscape while the tablet was still set up like a laptop, you would be looking at the screen upside-down. Similarly, secondary portrait is a 180-degree rotation of primary portrait. Once you select the portrait orientation you prefer for your tablet, tap Apply, and the screen will change.

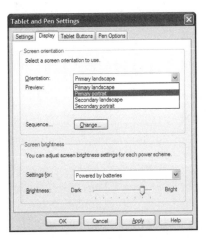

Figure 1-2   The Tablet And Pen Settings control panel lets you select one of four screen orientations.

■   **Use the Change Tablet And Pen Settings icon in the notification area**   This is a faster way to switch the screen orientation. Single-tap or right-tap on the **Change Tablet And Pen Settings** icon and select Change Screen Orientation from the shortcut menu shown in Figure 1-3. The screen will switch to the next of the four possible orientations set in the control panel. Continue to switch until you see the screen orientation you want. If you don't want to use all four possible screen orientations regularly, go to the Display tab in the Tablet And Pen Settings control panel and tap the Change button next to Sequence. Select the orientations you want in the order you want them to appear and set the remaining options to (None). If you have only two options chosen, as most people will, the Change Screen Orientation command will toggle between those two.

> **Tip**   Change Tablet And Pen Settings also lets you quickly toggle the speaker on and off (handy if you don't want to bother your neighbor on the airplane) and turn the screen off to save battery power. The Properties item takes you directly to the Tablet And Pen settings control panel.

Figure 1-3 Change Tablet And Pen Settings in the notification area gives quick access to commonly used commands.

■ **Use the hardware buttons, if available** This is fastest way to switch the screen orientation, but not all tablets have these buttons. If your tablet has hardware buttons, there will be a Tablet Buttons tab in the Tablet And Pen Settings control panel. This tab allows you to assign any number of functions or keystrokes to buttons on the face of the tablet. Often, Change Screen Orientation will be set as the default for one of the buttons. As with Change Screen Orientation on Change Tablet And Pen Settings, the hardware button scrolls through all the available screen orientations as set in the Tablet And Pen Settings control panel.

> **Tip** The primary landscape orientation usually puts the hardware buttons near the user's right hand. Left-handed users can switch this by activating the secondary portrait orientation instead of the primary one.

Using a Pen in Lieu of a Mouse

Until using your pen instead of a mouse is second nature, you can't really enjoy your tablet. One fundamental skill is moving the cursor. The pen should not make contact with the screen if you only want to move the cursor. In fact, as soon as the pen gets close enough to the screen, the cursor will jump to the pen's position, so you rarely need to move the cursor around the screen as you did with a mouse. Just to get a feel for the pen, though, try moving the cursor to various items on the screen, such as the Start menu, and hovering in place until the ToolTip comment appears.

> **Glossary**   To *hover* with your pen is to bring your pen close enough to the screen to move the cursor but not actually touch the screen. Hovering allows you to control the cursor without the risk of an accidental tap or drag.

When the pen does make contact with the screen, that is the equivalent of a click with the left mouse button, so you must make contact to tap (click) or drag. The key to a good tap or drag is tapping hard enough for the screen to register the contact but not pressing down excessively. This comes quickly with a little hands-on experience. As you practice, here are some tips for successful mousing with a pen and the logic behind them.

■ **Rest your hand on the screen**   This is counter-intuitive to anyone who has used a Palm Pilot or a Pocket PC, where the screen is touch-sensitive. Because it's the pen of the tablet that is sensitive, not the screen, you can rest your hand with no adverse effects. It is much more comfortable and easy to use the pen if you rest your hand.

> **Tip**   Clean your screen often. When you rest your hand on the screen it gets dirty quite quickly. Many office supply outlets and computer stores sell anti-static wipes for cleaning computer monitors that work very well.

■ **Hold the pen like a regular pen**   Resist the urge to hold the pen like a pointer. However you hold a real pen is the way to hold the tablet pen.

■ **Press firmly and tap with gusto**   The screen on your tablet is built for writing. You can't break it with the pen. Press firmly when you write and tap with a hard, short whack. As you get used to the tablet, press and tap with less pressure until you find the amount that works best for you.

- **Watch the cursor, not the pen** Particularly, watch the point of the cursor arrow. The alignment between the pen tip and the cursor is good but not perfect. If you tap an icon and nothing happens, the most likely cause is that the pen is over the icon, but the cursor is a bit off. It's the position of the cursor on the screen, not the pen, that ultimately matters to the computer.

- **Get a better pen** If your tablet came with a small stylus instead of a full-size pen, invest in a more comfortable pen. The more comfortable the pen, the easier it is to use. I've also noticed that some pens seem to have better cursor alignment than others. If you aren't happy with your pen, try others until you find one that works well for you. Make sure you get a pen that works with your particular tablet. See the sidebar on "How the Pen Works" for more information.

> **Tip** If you're having continued trouble getting your pen to work and you already tried tapping harder, try holding the pen more upright. This will improve the alignment between the pen tip and the cursor. Sometimes, when the pen is at a serious angle, the cursor is off to one side, almost as if it is a "shadow" cast by the pen. Also, the tip of the pen must compress slightly to send a signal. If the pen is held at too much of an angle, the tip will slide over the screen rather than compress.

Using a Pen for Right-Click and Right-Drag

Research shows only about 30% of Windows users ever use their right mouse button. This is too bad, since a right-click gives you instant access to context-sensitive shortcut menus full of useful commands. On a tablet, these menus save perhaps even more time and effort, so you should definitely know how to right-tap and right-drag. To get a good right-tap, hold the pen down longer until the right-tap icon appears and then lift the pen completely off the screen. Next highlight the desired item on the shortcut menu while hovering. Finally, tap the selected menu item.

> **Caution** It's very easy to accidentally select the wrong item on a shortcut menu if you keep the pen in contact with the screen after the shortcut menu appears.

How the Pen Works

There are actually two different pen digitizing systems used on tablets. They both accomplish the same task, but they do it slightly differently and provide different advantages and disadvantages.

Tablets incorporating the Finepoint digitizer use a battery-powered pen and a passive screen. The pen emits a directional magnetic field that induces a small electrical current in a sensor behind the screen that determines the pen's position. In addition, there's a pressure sensor in the pen that determines whether the pen is in contact with the screen. Tablets made with Wacom digitizers use a passive pen and an active screen. In this setup, the screen emits a weak magnetic field that induces an electrical current in the pen that, in turn, interferes with the magnetic field in the screen. The Wacom digitizers interpret this interference to determine the position of the pen. The pressure sensors in Wacom pens are also variable. They can tell when you are pressing lightly and when you are pressing hard. Finepoint sensors simply know that you are pressing down. If the option to enable pressure sensitivity is greyed-out in an application such as Windows Journal, you probably have a Finepoint pen. As you might imagine, a Finepoint pen will not work with a Wacom tablet nor will a Wacom pen work on a Finepoint tablet.

Is one better than the other? It depends on your needs. They sense the pen position with about equal accuracy. The Finepoint system has the distinct advantage that the passive screen does not draw power from the tablet battery, so the battery will not run down as quickly. The downside is that your pen battery makes the pen heavier and it will eventually run out and need replacement. The Wacom system might draw more power, but the pens are lighter, and I personally like the pressure sensitivity. If you're using your tablet for any real artistic work, pressure sensitivity is a must. Some Wacom pens have an additional cool feature called top of pen erase. These pens have a plastic "eraser" on them that's really a button. Flip the pen over and press down as you rub the screen, and you can erase your pen strokes. This feature is so intuitive and handy that I use it all the time.

If you haven't yet purchased your tablet, you might want to find out which pen system the tablets you are considering use. If you are planning to upgrade or replace your pen, make sure you know which system your tablet uses. The sure-fire way to know is if your pen has a battery, it's a Finepoint.

Pens with a button for a right-tap make the process quicker and easier. To right-tap with a pen button, hold the pen button down before you make contact with the screen, tap the point where you want to right-tap, and lift the pen back off the screen before releasing the pen button. The right-tap menu will appear where you tapped. The pen button is also the only easy way to right-drag on a tablet, such as you might do when you wanted to move a file from one folder to another rather than copying it. To right-drag, hold the pen button down before you make contact with the screen, press down and drag the item you want to move. Lift the pen off the screen before you release the pen button, and the shortcut menu will appear over the icon you just dragged. The disadvantage to using the pen button is that if you move the pen laterally too much as you right tap, you can accidentally right-drag and get the wrong shortcut menu. If this happens, tap anywhere on the screen other than the menu. If it happens to you often, try changing the pen tolerances in the Tablet And Pen Settings control panel.

Using the Built-In Tablet Tutorials

The Welcome To Tablet Computing tutorial only launches the first time you use your tablet. There are four more built-in tutorials that provide an overview of tablet computing and introductions to Input Panel, Windows Journal, and Speech input. The tutorial home, shown in Figure 1-4, will appear every time you start up your tablet until you tell them to go away by checking Do Not Show Me This Again. If you want to run the tutorials after you check this box, go to the Start menu, tap All Programs, tap the Tablet PC folder, and tap Tablet PC Tutorials. We will cover Input Panel and Speech input in Chapter 2 and explore Windows Journal in Chapters 3 through 5. Some basic use of Input Panel is necessary to simply get going on the tablet, so, if you haven't done so already, view the video portions of Tablet PC Tutorial and Tablet PC Input Panel Tutorial. Ideally, do the exercises as well.

The key items to take away from these tutorials are:

■   Use your pen instead of a mouse.

■   Use Input Panel on a tablet where you would have used a keyboard to enter text on a standard computer. You may use script or printing, but use upper and lower case and write using the line as a guide.

■   Open Input Panel using the icon on the taskbar. Close it when you're not using it if you need more screen space.

■   Tap once in the spot you want the type to appear before you start writing in Input Panel.

■   To enter text using your handwriting, tap the Writing Pad tab on the lower left of Input Panel. Correct the text using the onscreen keys to the right of the writing area for cursor control and deleting mistakes.

■   If you get frustrated with the writing pad, switch to the Input Panel keyboard by tapping the Keyboard tab on the lower left of Input Panel.

That's enough to give you rudimentary text input with the pen. If you just can't wait to find out more, go ahead and skip to Chapter 2 and come back here once you're an Input Panel expert. If you want to put off using Input Panel entirely for a while and you have a USB keyboard, simply plug it into tablet and use a standard keyboard instead.

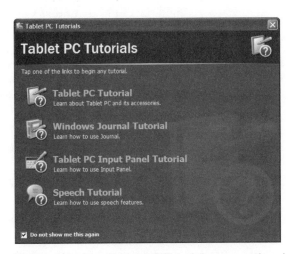

Figure 1-4   The Tablet PC Tutorials are worth going through at least once.

Note   Many of the peripherals on your tablet will use the Universal Serial Bus (USB). USB is easy to use, but there are a few things to be aware of. See Appendix A, Troubleshooting, if you are having trouble with USB peripherals.

Power Management

Power management issues are technically no different on the tablet than on any laptop. If there is a difference, it's simply that you're more likely to use the tablet on battery power and for longer periods of time. Here are some of the most useful ways for getting your batteries to last the longest. For a detailed discussion of power management under Windows XP, see Chapter 9, "Configuring Shutdown and Power Management Options" in the book, *Microsoft Windows XP Inside Out* (Microsoft Press: 2001).

Setting Power Options

The default power options settings for the tablet are a compromise between decent power savings and making your tablet behave similarly to a desktop or laptop computer. If you're willing to adjust these settings in the Power Options control panel, you can often squeeze an extra 15 to 30 minutes out of your battery life. Open the Power Options control panel by right-tapping on the Power/Battery icon in the notification area and selecting Adjust Power Properties or by using Control Panel. The control panel opens with the Power Schemes tab visible, as shown in Figure 1-5, which lets you set time of inactivity before the tablet invokes any of four power-saving actions:

- **Turn off monitor** On the tablet, the screen (monitor) backlight eats 40% of the power. Turning it off when you aren't using it is the single biggest power saver there is.

- **Turn off hard disks** The motors that spin your hard disk also use a sizable percentage of the power. Usually it's best to stop them when they're not needed. The only exception is if you're reading or writing large files (such as video or music) off the hard drive every few minutes. The power used to start the drive spinning is equal to the consumption during several minutes of steady operation.

- **System standby** Standby turns off the monitor, hard drive, and main processing functions of the tablet and consumes very little power. By design, all tablets must be able to resume from standby to full operation in 2 seconds or less, so having your tablet go in and out of standby often is no big deal.

- **System hibernates** Hibernation involves actually saving the contents of memory to the disk and shutting down. Once in hibernation, the tablet consumes no power, but it can take a minute or more to resume normal operation. When the tablet comes out of hibernation, all applications and any unsaved work are available, exactly as you left them.

> **Note**   Hibernation must be enabled on the Hibernate tab to appear as an option.

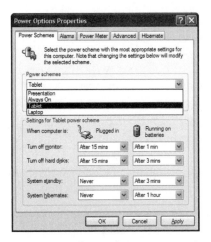

Figure 1-5   Power Schemes organizes four power-saving properties for use in different situations.

These power-conservation behaviors are organized for different situations. For example, you can make sure the screen normally turns off after one minute of inactivity but doesn't go blank at all when you are giving a presentation on battery power. There are quite a few power schemes by default, but none geared specifically for a tablet. Figure 1-5 shows custom settings for my tablet, in which the screen goes off after one minute and standby happens after three when running on batteries. Because the screen comes alive as soon as the pen gets near it, I hardly notice whether it's on or off, so I want it to happen as soon as possible. I set standby to a wait long enough that I can pause while working for a moment, but short enough that I don't waste power if I sit and think. Hibernate is set to one hour because I don't want the tablet to hibernate while I'm working, even during a long break, but I do want it to hibernate if I forget to turn it off. Notice that the settings are different for when I am plugged in and presumably working at my desk. The tablet switches between these two sets automatically when you plug into a power outlet and when you unplug again.

Tip   You can quickly switch between power schemes by single-tapping the **Power/Battery** icon in the notification area and selecting from a menu of all the saved power schemes. Since there are probably more power schemes in the system than you will ever need, deleting the ones you don't want makes this feature easier to use. If the Power/Battery icon is not visible in the notification area, you can add it by checking the Always Show Icon On The Taskbar check box on the Advanced tab of the Power Options control panel.

The Alarms tab and the Advanced tab are two other tabs in the Power Options control panel worth checking. The Alarms tab determines the actions taken at low and at critically low battery levels. Usually the defaults are fine, but you can adjust how much warning you get before you run out of power. You should ensure that when the tablet reaches a critical battery level, it either hibernates or shuts down to prevent you from losing your work. The Advanced tab has a check box for prompting for a password when resuming operation from standby. If you use standby often, uncheck this box. There is little point in a super-fast resume from standby if you must enter a password each time. Use the tablet security button to password-protect your tablet if you step away for a moment.

Tip   If you run on batteries for long periods, the best policy is to have a second battery. To switch batteries quickly, hibernate Windows and switch rather than shutting down and restarting. You should still save your work first.

Here are a few other items that help prolong battery life:

- **If possible, avoid hard drive and processor intensive activities while on batteries**   Complex graphics work, video editing, accessing large databases, and even playing music while you work will run down the batteries faster.

- **Turn off wireless networking whenever you aren't using it**   Wireless networking uses power whenever it is connected, whether you are actively using the network or not. In fact, weak batteries are sometimes the culprit if your tablet keeps dropping off a wireless network.

■ **Turn off shadow and transparency visual effects**   While these effects make application windows more pleasant to view, they are processor intensive. To turn off selected visual effects, open System Properties by right-tapping on My Computer and selecting Properties or by opening the System control panel. Tap the Advanced tab and in the Performance area tap Settings. By default, all the visual settings are active. Disabling the fade, slide, and shadow effects, as shown in Figure 1-6, reduce the processor load without changing the look of Windows too much. You might want to keep the Show Shadows Under Mouse Pointer turned on as it makes the mouse easier to see in bright light and outdoors.

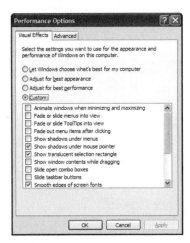

Figure 1-6   Simplifying the visual setting can help prolong battery life.

Recharging Batteries—What to Do

There was a time when most rechargeable batteries were made with nickel and cadmium, so-called NiCad batteries. These batteries had the unfortunate property that if you did not run them down all the way before recharging them, they would develop a "memory" and not recharge fully in the future. Most modern rechargeable batteries are nickel metal-hydride (NiMH) or lithium ion (Lion) batteries, which have much less of a memory problem and can be periodically refreshed if a problem does occur. While you should follow your manufacturer's recommendation for recharging your batteries, it's usually the best policy to plug in your tablet whenever you can.

Configuring Your Workspace

Perhaps more than any other computer, tablets are very personalized machines. Throughout the book, I'll offer suggestions for getting the most out of specific applications, but here are a few global suggestions that may help you use your tablet more effectively. All of these items are matters of personal choice. Try them out and keep the ones that work best for you.

Adjust Text and Icon Size

Ideally, you will be able to keep the text and icons on your tablet at the standard size to make the most of the limited screen space inherent in a portable computer. If you are having trouble seeing the icons and on-screen buttons on your tablet, however, you can adjust the dots per inch, or DPI, setting and increase the size of most of your icons and on-screen text. First close any programs you have running, and switch your tablet to a landscape screen orientation. Open the Display control panel, and tap the Settings tab. Tap the Advanced button to see the General settings shown in Figure 1-7. Change the DPI setting from 96 DPI to 120 DPI, and tap OK. You will have to restart your tablet to apply the new settings. The increase in size is only 20%, but it can make a big difference. The downside is that the screen will seem a bit more crowded, but it should still be usable.

Figure 1-7   If you have trouble tapping icons that are too small or reading the names of folders, you can increase their size.

Customize Your Start Menu

Navigating hierarchical menus such as the Start menu with a pen is a bit slower than navigating with a mouse, since you must lift the pen after each tap to see the next submenu. Customizing the Start menu using the Taskbar And Start Menu control panel can help by putting the most common items only two taps away. The control panel also provides some advanced options for adding recently used documents and favorites to the Start menu. Open the Taskbar And Start Menu control panel by right-tapping on the taskbar and selecting Properties or by using Control Panel. Tap the Start Menu tab, and tap Customize. The dialog box shown in Figure 1-8 appears with three basic options.

> **Tip**   When using the Start menu, tap to open each submenu rather than hovering and waiting for the menu to expand on its own.

Figure 1-8   Small icons and a greater number of recently used programs help make the most of your Start menu.

■   **Large icons vs. Small icons**   Switching to small icons lets you put more items in the Start menu without it taking over the entire screen. The text titles do not change size, so readability does not change.

- **Number of Programs on Start menu**   Windows XP keeps track of your most recently used programs and keeps them on the first level of the Start menu for quick access. By increasing the number of programs in this list, you can save time drilling down through several menus.

- **Show Internet and E-mail on Start menu**   Checking these items permanently places, or pins, your chosen Web browser and e-mail in the Start menu for easy access. Pinned items appear above the list of recently used items.

Adding Items to the Start Menu

Permanently adding, or pinning, items to the Start menu is a new feature in Windows XP. The idea is similar to the recently used items list, except pinned items will always be there. Pinned items are automatically excluded from the recently used list, so if you pin Word to the Start menu it will not appear in the list of recent programs. To pin a program to your Start menu, find the program anywhere on your computer—on the desktop, in the All Programs menu, or in Windows Explorer—and drag the icon to the Start menu. It will automatically appear in the pinned items list. Alternatively, you can right-tap that icon and select Pin To Start Menu from the shortcut menu.

> **Note**   If you prefer to use the Classic-style Start menu, select Classic Start Menu on the Start Menu tab of the Tablet And Pen Settings control panel. The new Windows XP Start menu features such as pinning, however, will no longer be available.

Customizing the Tablet Taskbar

While you should definitely set up your tablet in the way that is most comfortable to you, there are a few things you might want to do a bit differently because of the differences between pen input and a conventional mouse and to conserve space. To adjust any of these settings, right-tap anywhere in the taskbar and select Properties from the shortcut menu or open the Start Menu And Taskbar control panel.

■ **Put Items on the Quick Launch bar**   Many people use the Quick Launch bar icons as a way to launch Internet Explorer and their e-mail program and not much else. On a tablet, the Quick Launch bar allows for super-easy one-tap launching of your favorite programs. This is one less tap than the pinned items, but the icons are small and can be hard to see, especially in bright light or outdoors.

■ **Group Similar Items**   Windows XP allows you to group multiple windows belonging to one program. This feature is invaluable on the tablet, where the taskbar is usually restricted in size.

■ **Turn off autohide**   The autohide feature makes the taskbar disappear when not in use and reappear when you bring the cursor all the way to the edge of the screen. On many tablets, it's difficult to get the cursor far enough to the edge to unhide the taskbar reliably. The result is more frustration than it's worth. This is too bad, because screen real estate is very tight on the tablet, and a good way to autohide would help.

■ **Customize show/hide of notification area icons** Many people also ignore these small icons that usually sit in the lower right of the screen. Most of them you don't need to see on a regular basis, so you should set them to hide when inactive. Some of them you might want available all the time. For example, quick access to volume control can prevent embarrassment in a meeting when a reminder pops up while your boss is speaking. On the Taskbar tab of the Taskbar And Start Menu control panel, make sure the Hide Inactive Icons check box is checked and tap Customize to adjust these options.

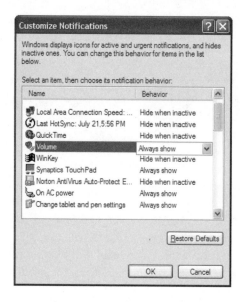

Tip   Most people know that tapping (clicking) a running program in the taskbar will maximize it, but many people don't know that tapping the taskbar icon a second time will minimize it. This feature provides a very handy way to switch back and forth between two running programs on the tablet. Windows XP also offers the handy option of closing a group of windows at once when you right-tap on a running program in the taskbar.

Radical Taskbars

This idea is a bit more radical, but I think it is well worth trying. Consider moving the taskbar to the top or side of the screen, instead of to the bottom, as shown in Figure 1-9. For right-handed pen users, reaching down to the bottom left of the screen for the taskbar Start button is somewhat awkward and when the Start menu pops up, you must lift your hand to see the menu items and then tap again. If you are drilling down through several folders, then you must do this several times. For left-handed users, the menu is visible, but the motion is even more awkward. Moving the taskbar to the top or side of the screen puts the Start button close to your resting hand and keeps the menus in view. While it might take a little getting used to, it's one of the most useful configuration changes you can make when using your tablet.

To move the taskbar, you must first ensure it is not locked. Right-tap in an area that does not contain any icons, and look at the shortcut menu. If there is a check next to Lock The Taskbar, select Lock The Taskbar and tap. The check will disappear. If the taskbar is already unlocked, tap anywhere outside the shortcut menu and it will close. Next tap an area that does not contain any icons, and drag the taskbar to the top or side of the screen. If you try the side, use the same side as your dominant hand. Nothing happens until the cursor gets close to the side of the screen, and then the taskbar will jump to the new position.

If you try the side position, the taskbar will be fairly wide. To make it narrower, hover your pen near the border between the taskbar and the rest of the desktop and adjust the position until you see a double-headed arrow. Drag the border of the taskbar towards the edge of the screen until it is the width you want. The word *Start* will disappear off the Start button, but the menu will still work. Horizontal space on the tablet is precious, so if you use a side taskbar, you want to make it as narrow as is comfortable. Losing horizontal space is the biggest drawback of the side taskbar, but the length of it allows you to see many Quick Launch bar icons for easy program launching and many open documents all at once. Having the taskbar on the top keeps the full screen width available for your applications and is a little easier to get used to. Try each setting for a few days and see how well they work for you.

Figure 1-9 A top or side taskbar is much more comfortable on a tablet once you get used to it.

One other potential drawback is that when you switch to landscape view, as will happen when you work in laptop mode or when connected to an external monitor and keyboard, the taskbar will still be on the top or side. You can either move it back to the bottom of the screen when you switch to landscape mode or keep it in the new position and see what you think. I like the side taskbar in landscape mode because the documents I work on are longer than they are wide, and I have lots of unused real estate on the sides of my monitor anyway. Having the taskbar on the side gives you maximum vertical space while giving full access to all the taskbar features—and without the need for auto hide.

Controlling Tablet and Pen Settings

You might want to use your tablet for a while before you change the default pen options, but taking a little time to customize your tablet and pen settings is well worth the effort. Not only will you get better results while using your pen, you will have a better idea how the tablet interprets and responds to your pen inputs. You will probably need to come back a few times to get your settings just right.

"The default [pen] settings are good for the novice user. We expect people to want to change the settings after a month."
–Anoo Padte, Tablet PC Team

Calibration

Open the Tablet And Pen Settings control panel from the Printers And Other Hardware group or by selecting Properties from Change Tablet And Pen Settings in the notification area. The control panel opens with the Settings tab selected as shown in Figure 1-10. The Settings tab has a calibration tool to calibrate the accuracy of your pen. The calibration tool is a bit limited in that it samples only four points on the screen, but it's still the best way to make the cursor move where you want it to using the pen. To begin the calibration process, tap the Calibrate button. Calibrate the screen for both landscape and portrait orientations. When you calibrate, keep your head in the same position it is in when you use your tablet. The whole point of calibration is to adjust for your personal perspective between pen and screen. Use your tablet for a while to see how well the pen directs the cursor, allowing for a bit of lag time between them. If the cursor isn't following the pen well over the entire screen, try holding your pen more upright. If the cursor seems to be following the pen fine over most of the screen, but has a problem area, try adjusting the calibration again. The Settings tab also controls the "handedness" of your tablet, but that should have been set when you went through the Welcome To Tablet Computing tutorial. The handedness determines both the way the tablet interprets certain characters in Input Panel and on which side of the cursor menus appear.

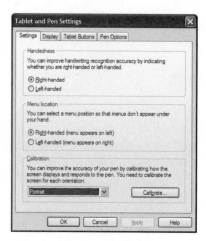

Figure 1-10   Customizing the calibration of your screen can improve
pen-instead-of-mouse accuracy.

Caution   During calibration, if you accidentally tap the screen somewhere other than the target, you can end up with a cursor that's difficult
to control. Tap Cancel to end the calibration without saving the changes,
and then calibrate the pen again. If you noticed too late and now can't
control the pen, use the touch pad if available or hook up an external
USB mouse to control the cursor and launch the calibration again.

Display Settings

We already looked at the display settings in Figure 1-2. The Display tab also lets
you set the screen brightness for when the tablet is plugged in and when it is
operating on batteries. While it is true that the screen brightness affects battery
life, in practice you must manually adjust your screen brightness on a tablet as
you move from office to conference room to outdoors to adjust for different
lighting, so the setting here is fairly irrelevant.

Hardware Buttons

The Tablet Buttons tab, shown in Figure 1-11, lets you configure your hardware
buttons to perform many different actions or to enter common keyboard commands. The default settings for these buttons are probably fine for most users,
but you might wish to customize them for your own needs. Figure 1-11 shows

a custom set I used for writing this book. Two of the buttons are set to quickly take screen shots for this book and another is set to turn the screen off manually. Having one-button control of the screen allowed me to turn it off and save power during interviews with the Tablet PC team without looking down. Notice that the hardware buttons on this tablet included a function button, similar to a Shift key, that allowed defining two actions for each hardware button.

Figure 1-11   Tablet buttons give you access to your most needed keyboard commands.

> **Tip**   Pressing the function hardware button twice displays the Change Tablet And Pen Settings menu, providing quick access to Change Screen Orientation, Turn Off Screen, and Turn Speaker On Or Off. If your tablet has only a few hardware buttons, this shortcut frees the remaining hardware buttons to use for other commands that are very handy, such as Delete.

By default, hardware buttons are the same for all screen orientations, but they can be set for different functions depending on the screen orientation. Customizing the buttons for common commands such as Up, Down, and Enter is useful when in tablet mode, but these are not needed if your keyboard is available, as it often is in primary landscape mode. You can change the functions of these buttons so that when you are in landscape mode, they launch often-used programs or let you easily perform common actions, such as skipping to the next track on your music CD. To create a custom hardware button set for a particular orientation, first select the orientation you want from the drop-down list in the top half of the Tablet Buttons tab of the Tablet And Pen Settings control panel. Next select the hardware button you want to change and tap Change. Select the command you want for that hardware button from the drop-down list as shown in Figure 1-12, and tap OK. To set a hardware button so that it will enter a keyboard command, such as Delete, choose Press A Key Or Key Combination and enter the key combination using the on-screen keyboard. You might also select any application on your computer so that it launches with the touch of a hardware button. Usually icons on the Quick Launch bar are a better option for easily opening programs.

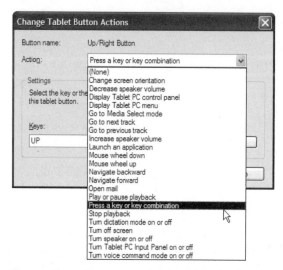

Figure 1-12   You can customize tablet hardware buttons to meet your specific needs.

Pen Options

The Pen Options tab allows you to customize the pen behavior to match your expectations and is helpful if you aren't getting a good right-tap. First-time tablet users are often frustrated when they accidentally press the pen button and get shortcut menus where they don't expect them. You can disable the pen button by unchecking the Use Pen Button To Right-Click check box shown in Figure 1-13.

You will still be able to right-click by using the pen to press and hold, but you will no longer be able to right-drag. Unless you use right-drag often, this is a helpful change for many people. By default, the wait for a shortcut menu when you press and hold is annoyingly long and, because you must lift your pen to see the menu, it sometimes disappears before you can find and tap your selection. To adjust these properties, select the Press And Hold pen action and tap the Settings button. Adjust the sliders so that the right-click mode activation is shorter and the press and hold duration is longer as shown in Figure 1-14. You can test your settings on the light bulb animation but trying the new settings in the programs you use most is more telling. If you like the pen button and want to disable press and hold, uncheck the Enable Press And Hold For Right-Click check box in the Press And Hold Settings dialog box.

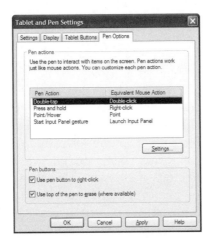

Figure 1-13   Customizing your pen options is essential for reliable pen input.

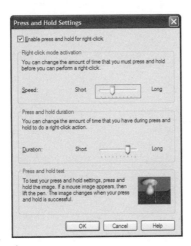

Figure 1-14   Customizing your press and hold options.

> **Tip** Some pens with pen buttons have a combination button that acts as a right-click if pushed one way and an eraser if pressed a different way. Use Top Of The Pen To Erase is enabled and disabled on the Pen Options tab and can be enabled independently of the pen button for right-tap.

The Pen Options tab also allows you to adjust your double-tap speed and spatial tolerance for double-tapping and point and hover used to get ToolTips to appear. The Double-Tap Settings dialog box is shown in Figure 1-15. Spatial tolerance determines how much your pen can move around in a confined area and still register as staying in one place. If you have the hands of a surgeon, then you can use a small spatial tolerance because your hand will tap twice in almost exactly the same spot. If you have had one too many cups of coffee, then you will need a large spatial tolerance. The only disadvantage to a large spatial tolerance is that you might double-tap when you didn't mean to. If you are having problems with your double-tap, the most likely cause is that your second tap wasn't firm enough for the pen to sense. Think "woodpecker," and try double-tapping again. If that isn't the issue, you can increase your double-tap spatial tolerance and play with the double-tap speed. Test effects of different settings on the animated door until you can make it open and close with 100% accuracy. If your ToolTip menus keep disappearing before you can read them, increasing the spatial tolerance should correct the problem.

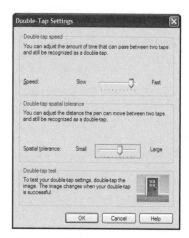

Figure 1-15 Customizing your double-tap speed and spatial tolerance.

> **Try This** Sometimes the best way to really understand a system is to experiment with its extremes. Try setting your press and hold, double-tap, and spatial tolerance settings to one extreme and seeing how it affects your pen. Now go back and try the other extreme. This should give you a better feel for what each control actually does and allow you to fine tune them to your needs.

Press and Hold Conflicts

There are a few situations in which press and hold for right-tap is a problem. The most common conflict occurs when dragging a scroll bar to scroll through a document. If you press and hold on the scroll bar but wait too long to start scrolling, you will get a shortcut menu. Another conflict occurs with some programs using floating tool palettes, such as Adobe Photoshop, where you must press and hold to change or select items on the palette. If your tablet's press and hold is active, you might not be able to use the tool palette fully. If you are having conflicts, try increasing the delay for press and hold or turning it off. You might also notice that on-screen buttons, such as the New, Open, and Save buttons near the menus in Word, do not appear to press down on your tablet. This is because the animation for button pressing is incompatible with press and hold. If you disable press and hold, the on-screen button animation will work again. The button-animation conflict is strictly a matter of visual preference; the buttons will still work even if they are not animated.

Key Points

- Use your pen for all mouse work, including left and right mouse buttons.
- Customize your Taskbar And Start Menu control panel for maximum utility.
- Customize your Tablet And Pen Settings control panel to meet your personal needs and work style.

2

Tablet PC Input Panel and Ink

The Tablet PC Input Panel is primarily a tool for entering text when a standard keyboard is not convenient or available. This, of course, is something you must do all the time on a tablet, so Input Panel is a large part of your tablet experience. Ideally, you could use your pen and enter information directly into any document by putting the pen to the screen where you want the information to go and starting to write. In fact, this was the original plan for pen input and may be possible as more programs appear specifically designed for the tablet. The problem is that the majority of programs you use on your tablet today were designed for keyboard input, not for pen input. The first attempts at making keyboard-centric programs accept pen input directly worked, but the process was confusing for the user. The solution was to create a system in which the users could place the cursor where they wanted to write but actually write the information with a pen in a separate input area, much like the writing area of a Palm or Pocket PC. The computer would respond as if the user had placed the cursor with a mouse and started typing on a keyboard. That system is Input Panel.

Why Use Input Panel

While Input Panel has its limitations, it will work with every Microsoft Windows application that runs on the tablet, even command-line applications. Part of your success in using Input Panel is knowing which part of Input Panel to use for which situation and when not to use it at all. Each input option has its advantages, disadvantages, and best uses.

- **On-Screen Keyboard**   The on-screen keyboard is a tedious way to enter more than a short sentence worth of text. Since it actually is a keyboard, however, there are no handwriting recognition errors and symbols such as @ are easily accessible. The on-screen keyboard is best for entering passwords, Web addresses that are not real words, uncommon technical terms not found in the tablet's dictionary, and small on-screen text corrections.

- **Writing Pad**   The writing pad is best for entering up to four or five sentences of normal English. Exactly how many sentences varies with how well the handwriting recognizer understands your hand-writing and the language you use, as well as your tolerance for going back and correcting mistakes. The writing pad works well for short e-mail messages, Web addresses based on real words, minor docu-ment editing, and many general Windows tasks, such as naming new folders.

- **Write Anywhere**   Write Anywhere is a variation on the writing pad that provides more writing space and a transparent writing surface. The word recognition error rate is the same as with Input Panel but it is more comfortable to enter a paragraph or more of text with handwriting. It's somewhat harder to use your pen in place of a mouse while Write Anywhere is activated.

- **Speech Input**   Speech input is done through Input Panel and is good for text input of many paragraphs. It's fast, but it requires con-centration to avoid "ums" and "uhs" and time to go back and correct mistakes. Speech input frees you from typing or writing as you think, which can be helpful for getting your thoughts down if you don't type quickly, and it can be useful for transcribing documents if you're not a fast typist.

- **Standard Keyboard**   A standard keyboard is still the best tool for entering text quickly and accurately. To use your tablet fully, some kind of external keyboard is required at least some of the time.

Viewing and Using the Input Panel Keyboard

Most of the time you're using your tablet you'll want Input Panel hidden because it takes up quite a bit of screen space. To see Input Panel, tap the **Tab-let PC Input Panel** button on your taskbar. By default, Input Panel will appear at the bottom of your screen in keyboard mode as shown in Figure 2-1. To make Input Panel disappear, either tap the Input Panel button again or tap the close button in the upper right of the Input Panel window. When Input Panel is visible, you can enter text by tapping once on the screen to place your cursor and then tapping in your text using the on-screen keyboard.

Figure 2-1   Input Panel's primary function is to input text when a standard keyboard is not accessible.

Here's an example for entering text using the Input Panel keyboard. Open Microsoft Internet Explorer, and then open Input Panel. Tap once in the Address box of Internet Explorer to select the text. Using the Input Panel keyboard, enter the URL *www.microsoft.com/tabletpc/* using the Input Panel keyboard as shown in Figure 2-2. Tap the Enter key on the Input Panel keyboard when you are finished. If you're connected to the Internet, the Tablet PC home page should appear. Incidentally, this page is a great source of information, tips, and downloads for your Tablet PC. If the page doesn't load, try entering the full URL of *http://www.microsoft.com/windowsxp/tabletpc/*

Remember that using the Input Panel keyboard is just like using a standard keyboard in that you must specify where you want the text to go before you start typing. The most common mistake people make using Input Panel the first few times is forgetting to tap once on the screen to place the cursor.

If you make a mistake as you type, you can Backspace, Delete, and even use modifier keys, such as Ctrl+C for copy, just as you would with a standard keyboard. To use a modifier key, such as the Shift or Ctrl key, simply tap the modifier first and then tap the modified key. To make entering e-mail addresses a bit easier, the Input Panel keyboard has a dedicated @ key as well.

Tip   Keyboard commands, such as Ctrl+C for copy are cumbersome to enter on the Input Panel keyboard. Tap buttons or use the menus instead of the Input Panel keyboard.

Figure 2-2   Use the Input Panel keyboard to enter text as well as keyboard commands such as Enter, Tab, and Delete.

The Input Panel keyboard has a few shortcomings. It lacks a number pad, and it's fairly easy to tap the wrong key inadvertently if the keys are resized too small. If you use an alternative keyboard layout, such as a French or German keyboard, the keys on Input Panel do not appear to change even though they actually create different characters when you type them. If any of these are a problem for you, use the on-screen keyboard built into every version of Windows XP. The on-screen keyboard is found in the Accessibility folder in the Accessories folder in the Start menu. If you use this keyboard often, you can drag the icon to your Quick Launch bar or to your Start menu for easy access. Figure 2-3 shows the Windows on-screen keyboard and the Input Panel keyboard.

Figure 2-3   Use the Windows on-screen keyboard (upper) for alternative keyboard layouts, such as this French layout, and for access to a number pad.

Adjusting Input Panel Appearance and Position

There are a couple of ways to make Input Panel a little more space-efficient on your screen. If you don't mind tapping smaller keys, you can resize Input Panel. You can also enlarge Input Panel to make it easier to tap keys if you want. You might actually find it easier to type text if your keyboard is smaller because you won't have to move your hand as far to get from one end of the keyboard to the other.

You can also undock Input Panel so that it becomes a floating toolbar. While docked, Input Panel appears at the bottom of your screen, and any open windows are resized to fit the remaining space. The undocked Input Panel floats on top of other windows, so you may drag it anywhere you want on the screen, though it might obscure some of the window you are using. While undocked, Input Panel can be resized for width as well as height and can be made quite small. To toggle Input Panel docking on and off, tap the Input Panel Tools menu and select Dock. As with pen preferences, whether to use a docked or undocked Input Panel is really a matter of personal preference. Some people like having Input Panel next to the area of the screen where they are entering text; others like having it always on the bottom. Try both and see which works best for you.

Tip   Double-tapping the Input Panel title bar will quickly dock and undock Input Panel.

Whether Input Panel is docked or not, you can hide most of it so that only the title bar appears by tapping the **Hide Pen Input Area** button (arrow) on the title bar. If Input Panel is docked, it will retreat to the very bottom of the screen. If it is undocked, the title bar will continue to float, but Input Panel will disappear. While this feature may be useful in certain situations, in general it is just as simple to close Input Panel between uses and have it completely out of your way. It opens and closes instantly and can do so an infinite number of times without causing system problems.

A really cool way to make Input Panel appear is with the open Input Panel gesture. To open Input Panel this way, move your pen back and forth rapidly several times just above the screen but without actually touching it. The motion can be horizontal, vertical, or on a slant, so long as it is rapid and the pen is not in contact with the screen. The motion is also quite large by default, as shown in Figure 2-4, but can be changed in the Tablet And Pen Settings control panel on the Pen Options tab. If Input Panel was docked when it was last closed, it opens still docked. If it was undocked, it appears wherever you made the gesture. This feature is really handy because you can open and use Input Panel without moving your pen to a different part of the screen.

Glossary   A *gesture* is any pen action designed to send a command to the computer that isn't a mouse movement or a text entry. Right-tap is also considered a gesture.

Tip   Make the open Input Panel gesture slightly below the area where you want to enter information so that it doesn't cover the place your text will appear.

Figure 2-4   The open Input Panel gesture. It can be made in any direction, anywhere on the screen.

Using the Input Panel Writing Pad

The Input Panel writing pad accomplishes exactly the same thing as the on-screen keyboard, entering text when a standard keyboard is not available, but it uses your handwriting as the source for the text. The system for handwriting recognition used on your tablet is the culmination of years of research and is quite arguably the best in the business, but it will make mistakes. The key to satisfaction with the Input Panel writing pad is understanding how to minimize those mistakes, correct them easily where they occur, and use alternative means of text input where the writing pad doesn't meet your needs.

Handwriting Recognition Errors

Our tolerance for errors in actual handwriting is much higher than in print. When you read a quick handwritten note from a friend that says: "Meet me in front of the post office" and the word "office" isn't quite legible, you barely notice because you understood the message. Compare that to getting an e-mail message that says: "Meet me in front of the post offer." Now your friend seems rushed or careless, even though you understood the same percentage of the message as with the handwritten note.

My Handwriting: I promise honesty

Writing this book presented me with a serious philosophical question: Do I show readers my real handwriting? The truth is I have terrible handwriting when I print and even worse handwriting in cursive. In fact, my cursive is so bad the tablet can't read it, most humans can't read it, and often I can't read it unless I remember what I was thinking at that moment. My printing is passable.

So I had to decide whether I should intentionally print neatly for this book or whether I should show a real person's handwriting and the tablet's actual interpretation of that handwriting. I chose the latter (as you can probably tell by looking at the figures). All the handwriting screen shots you see were written at my normal speed and the interpreted text was what the tablet generated on the first attempt, except for situations in which I needed a recognition error for an example and it took more than one try to get one.

Entering Text with Handwriting

To switch to the writing pad for text input, tap the Writing Pad tab on the bottom of Input Panel. To test out the writing pad, you will need somewhere for the text to go. The best choice is a word processor, such as Microsoft Word, or a text editor such as Notepad.

Figure 2-5 shows an Input Panel writing example and the resulting text. As promised in the sidebar, "My Handwriting: I promise honesty," the text shown in Notepad is the actual text as recognized by the tablet.

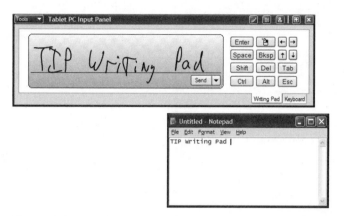

Figure 2-5   As with the Input Panel keyboard, place the cursor where you want the text to appear before writing on the Input Panel writing pad.

Take a close look at the word "Writing" as I have written it in Figure 2-5. My "t" has an extra line where I dragged my pen up to cross it rather than lifting the pen and my "g" looks more like a "y" because I did not close it off. Also, my "d" in "Pad" resembles a cursive "l" or perhaps an "el." The tablet correctly interpreted what I wrote, despite these shortcomings, because it doesn't simply interpret single letters, it looks at the individual letters and the whole word. Even though my "g" looks like a "y," the recognition system correctly understood "Writing" because "Writiny" is not a word. The system of identifying both letters and entire words can work for or against you depending on how you write. Table 2-1 provides some general rules, examples of how the errors might look on the screen, and the results on handwriting recognition. Some of the items in the table may seem especially dramatic, but the truth is that most took two or three attempts to get an error at all.

Table 2-1 **Some basic rules to greatly reduce recognition errors.**

Writing Pad Input	Resulting Text	Notes
	TABLE+ Tablet	Upper and lower-case work better than all capitals.
	Tablet Fillet	Cursive works better than printing if your cursive is fairly neat and even.
	Watch yours pacing	Leave space between words.
	On the line forth.live	Write on the line.
	Total/ t.our,'de	Use a normal height to width ratio, particularly when printing

The Send Button

When you first try out the writing pad, you'll probably find yourself waiting at the end of each line for the text to disappear from the pad and appear in your document. This is not because the handwriting recognizer is slow. In fact, the recognizer has the word interpreted in a fraction of a second. The speed at which the words disappear off the pad is determined by the Input Panel options. These options are described later in this chapter in "Setting Input Panel Options." If you find yourself waiting for Input Panel to empty, tap the Send button sitting just below the writing line and your wait will be over.

How Handwriting Recognition Works

The handwriting recognition system on your tablet is the culmination of years of work and analysis of literally millions of handwriting samples. The resulting system is sophisticated enough that it is referred to as a *neural net*. Rather than simply trying to translate the ink strokes you write into letters and words, it uses several information sources to determine your intentions. For example, when you write "ing" on the writing pad the recognition system creates several possible interpretations. You might be adding a suffix to a word, trying to write "ivy" with sloppy letters, or writing "ing" as a word all by itself. Factors that go into the decision are how you wrote the word (block letters or cursive), capitalization, similar words in the tablet dictionaries, grammar rules, words near the cursor, and more. Sometimes it even knows the type of information the application getting the text is expecting and will weight its decision accordingly. Using our "ing" example, if the cursor is at the end of the word "walk" then the system is more likely to choose adding "ing." If the cursor had been at the end of "banana" the system would be more likely to insert a space and then the word "ivy" because "walking" is a word and "bananaing" is not. Of course that would be just one component of the decision among many.

The result is that the system will make different choices as to what it thinks you wanted to say depending on the circumstances. The process is too complicated to second-guess, but as you work you will learn how it responds during your common tasks. If you note certain patterns that regularly result in the effect you wanted, you can adjust your writing habits to create that same situation in the future.

> **Tip**   Even though it's called "Send," this Send button has nothing to do with e-mail; it just sends what it reads to the current program. Don't tap Enter on Input Panel instead of Send. That will send the text *and* send an Enter command. If you were writing a filename in a Save dialog box when this happened, the file would save before you could see and correct the filename.

Correcting Recognition Errors

By default, a few keyboard keys appear beside the writing pad. This is the quick keys pad; it's helpful for putting returns and tabs into a document along with the writing pad text. The quick keys pad also provides arrow, Backspace, Delete, and Space keys for making simple corrections. To correct text, either tap next to the mistake to place the cursor and use the Backspace or Delete keys or select the mistake with the pen and rewrite it using the writing pad or the Input Panel keyboard. Normally the handwriting recognition looks for whole words; however, when you enter letters one at a time on the writing pad to correct text, the system knows you are correcting the word and won't try to make new words. It's even "smart" enough that if you add a suffix to a word, such as adding "ing" to "fly," it usually understands you are adding to a word rather than inserting a new one.

Fixing Symbols and Punctuation

Entering symbols such as _ and + in the writing pad can be very difficult. These symbols usually appear as E and t. The numbers 1 and 0 are also a challenge as they usually come out as the letters l and O. Tapping the **Symbols Pad** button (&) on the Input Panel title bar opens a palette of commonly used symbols as shown in Figure 2-6. The symbols pad closes automatically after you tap a single key. You may drag the symbols pad off the title bar and keep it available as a floating palette. This is called *tearing off* the palette. It will then remain visible until you close it or hide Input Panel.

> **Tip**   If you want more space on the writing pad, you can also add the quick keys pad to the Input Panel title bar as a button and remove the quick keys pad from the main Input Panel window. See "Setting Input Panel Options" later in this chapter for more information.

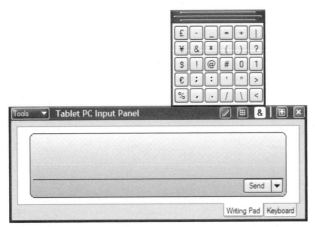

Figure 2-6   Entering common symbols from the symbols pad saves a lot of frustration.

Using Text Preview

The text preview pane lets you view and edit text after it's converted from handwriting but before it's inserted into a document. To view the text preview pane, tap the Tools menu on Input Panel and select Text Preview. The text preview pane will appear above Input Panel. Now when you write on the writing pad, the interpreted text appears in the text preview pane rather than in a Windows application. To send the text from the text preview pane into an application, tap once in the application where you want the text to go and then tap the Send Text button in the text preview pane. Figure 2-7 shows this process.

Figure 2-7   The text preview pane lets you see and, if necessary, edit the recognized text before it goes out to the Windows application.

> **Note**   If text appears in the text preview pane but the Send Text button is grayed out, you probably haven't placed the cursor telling Input Panel where you want the text to go.

Alternate Words List

While the text is in the text preview pane, you have an additional tool for text correction. The handwriting recognition system inserts its best guess for your word in the text preview pane. It also keeps on file up to ten more words that are strong alternate possibilities. Single-tap or double-tap any word in the text preview pane, and a small green carat appears on the upper left of the word. Tap the carat, and a list of alternate words appears. In Figure 2-8, the text "Alternate Words List" was recognized as "Alternate Wards List," but the correct word was on the list of alternates. Words capitalized incorrectly is one of the most common handwriting recognition problems in Input Panel. You'll notice that the first alternate in the list will always be the same word, but with opposite capitalization. The alternate words list functions like most spelling checkers. Select the correct word from the list, and it replaces the original. A small version of the original ink also appears in case you can't remember what you wrote. Even when the words chosen by the system seem way off, the correct words may still be on the alternates list. I had "tomorrow evening" come up as "terrarium every" once, but the correct word was available for both of them.

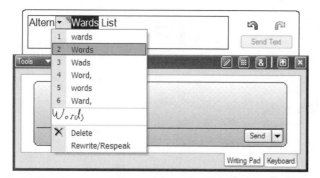

Figure 2-8   While text is still in the text preview pane, you can substitute from a list of alternates as well as perform drag and drop edits.

You may select many words at once or parts of a word to correct. Occasionally this allows you to correct two words at once but usually not, and the original ink does not appear with groups of words. Options to delete or rewrite the word also appear, but these are a bit superfluous. If you want to rewrite a word in the text preview pane, select it by double-tapping and write a new word on the writing pad. The new word will replace the old one. The text preview pane can hold many paragraphs' worth of text, and you can drag and drop to rearrange words.

Tip   With many applications, once the text leaves Input Panel the alternates list is lost. Some applications, however, such as Word 2002 (with the Microsoft Office XP Pack for Tablet PC installed), let you access the alternate words list even after the text is inserted into the document. If the application you are using has this type of pen integration, then the text preview pane serves little purpose.

Building the Dictionary

The writing pad will not learn your handwriting, but it can learn your vocabulary. Because recognizing the whole word is a major component of handwriting recognition, adding words to your dictionary is critical. At first you may be adding dozens of words a day, especially if your work involves technical or industry-specific terms. Stick with it. As you use your tablet, the frequency with which you add words will decline rapidly, and the tablet's ability to understand your writing will astound you.

Adding a word to the dictionary is a two-step process. First you must correct the word as it appears on screen. Once it's correct, you can add it to the dictionary. Figure 2-9 shows how the word *Hayabusa*, the Japanese word for *Peregrine*, was interpreted as *Hayabuga*. Presumably my "s" looked more like a "g." It's useful to note that the recognition system chose to use the letters as it saw them rather than making the letters into a dictionary word, such as *Hamburger*. This means there *were* no dictionary words close enough to the string of letters I wrote. Notice as well that the Add To Dictionary option appears for *Hayabuga*, in case it is a new word the tablet should learn. Once you correct the text, you can add it to the dictionary. In the future, the recognition system will substitute the real word *Hayabusa*, even when an "s" looks like a "g", because there is a real word that is very close.

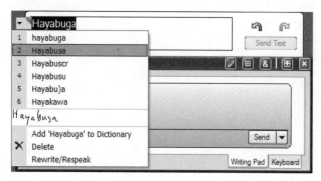

Figure 2-9 Choose the correct word from the list if it is available.

The option to add words to the dictionary can be a bit confusing. It only appears when you select a single word that is not already in the dictionary, yet sometimes it doesn't appear when you think it should. In Figure 2-10, the word "Jabberwocky" was interpreted as "Jabberw oh y" You can see the recognition system understood my letters fairly well, only mistaking a "ck" for an "h", but stumbled organizing them into words. Tapping the green carat shows a list of alternates, but no Add To Dictionary option appears because more than one word is selected. Because none of the alternates is close, we need to fix the word manually.

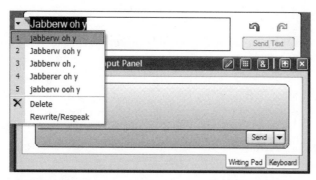

Figure 2-10 The word *Jabberwocky* was interpreted as multiple words, so Add To Dictionary is not an option.

You could tap the "oh" and hope "ock" is on the alternates list, and then use Backspace on the quick keys pad to take out the spaces. A faster way is to select the "oh" and the spaces on both sides and then write "ock" on the writing pad to replace it, as shown in Figure 2-11.

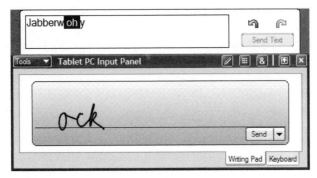

Figure 2-11   To close up the word, replace the center letter and the space on both sides.

Now that you have the single correct word, you can select it to add it to the dictionary. If you try this, however, you will not see an Add To Dictionary option, as shown in Figure 2-12. The reason is that both "Jabberwocky" and "jabberwocky" are already in the dictionary, as evidenced by the lowercase version in the alternate list. *Jabberwocky* didn't appear before now because the system thought the text was more than one word.

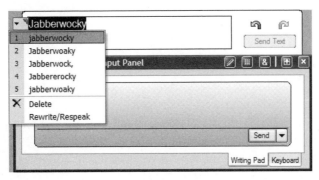

Figure 2-12   Once "Jabberwocky" is a complete word, we discover it actually was in the dictionary.

In addition to dictionary words, it's helpful to add strings of text you often use to the tablet dictionary, such as Web and e-mail addresses that you use frequently, abbreviations and slang that appear in your e-mail messages, and unusual names and places. Don't worry about overloading the dictionary.

> **Caution**   It's very tempting to add passwords to your dictionary so that you can write them quickly rather than tapping them out with a keyboard. Unfortunately, this is a security risk, as anyone with some technical savvy could open your dictionary and see all your passwords. Unless you don't care who might get at your password-protected data, don't save your passwords in the dictionary.

Previous and Next Text

The text preview pane also keeps a list of all the text you viewed in the window. If you want to enter the same text several times in a document, you can scroll back through a list of text strings you wrote using the arrow buttons (Recall Preview Text and Recall Next Text) on the right of the text preview pane, find the text you want, and tap Send Text. This applies only to text you wrote with the text preview pane open. Any text you wrote while text preview was closed is not saved.

More Writing Pad Tips

Here are a few more tips to help you get the most out of the writing pad:

- Because the ratio of height to width of letters is important, adjust the height of the Input Panel window so that you can write comfortably while still having your capital letters use about 7/8 of the writing area.

- If the handwriting recognizer keeps interpreting single words as many small words or individual letters, your letters are too far apart. Either make them closer together or use cursive handwriting.

- The longer the writing pad area relative to its height, the more words you can fit in before you run out of space.

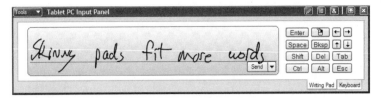

- The smaller you write, the closer together your letters should be. It's even okay if they occasionally overlap. This is especially important if you reconfigure your writing pad to show two lines instead of one line.

- If you use the writing pad to input full sentences on a regular basis, try decreasing the time before text automatically inserts or try a two-line writing pad. Either option allows you to write continuously without waiting for ink to disappear. See "Setting Input Panel Options" later in the chapter for more information on a two-line writing pad.

- To input long sections of text to older programs, fill the text preview pane with an entire message and then correct it all at once.

- If the system keeps misunderstanding a word, spell it out one letter at a time and then add it to the dictionary.

- For better results when correcting single letters, use cursive to create lowercase letters and print for uppercase. The one exception is capital I.

- Use a cursive for capital I and draw the upper hook and lower horizontal of a 1 (one) to distinguish them from l (el).

- To create an ampersand (&), you can write the common abbreviation of "E" with a vertical line through it.

- Write the http:// prefix for Web addresses.

- The writing pad often adds a space on the end of each word. This can cause a problem with some filenames, login names, and passwords. If you're having trouble with something that appears to be correct, try pressing Backspace to remove the last character after text appears. Capitalization errors can cause similar problems.

Writing Pad Gestures

There are four gestures that provide keystroke shortcuts while you are using the writing pad. These gestures are pen movements that will not be transformed into text. Instead, Input Panel will behave as if you tapped a button on the quick keys pad. Gestures work only on a blank writing pad, so you must wait until it is free of ink. You may use the gestures to control the cursor in a document or in the text preview pane. Gestures are sent immediately, so the ink will not stay in the Input Panel window for a moment before disappearing. If it does stay for a moment, then the gesture was misinterpreted as text.

Keystroke Gestures

The key to executing a good gesture is to do it fast and with authority. Timid gestures just don't work as well. Table 2-2 shows both a generic version of the gesture and an example of what this might look like on the writing pad. Notice how the Space and Backspace gestures use most of the pad area. This is not required, but it seems to give more consistent results.

> **Caution**   If you have text selected in the text preview pane or in a document and you make a gesture, the selected text will be deleted.

Table 2-2   **These four gestures allow quick keystrokes without using the quick keys pad or the Input Panel keyboard.**

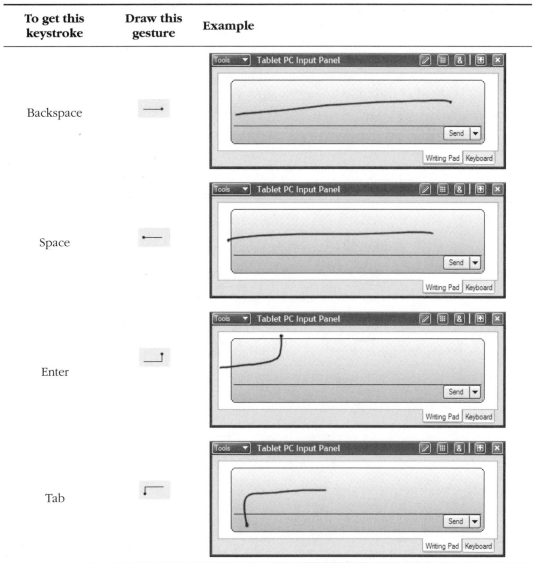

To get this keystroke	Draw this gesture	Example
Backspace		
Space		
Enter		
Tab		

Scratch-Out Gesture

In contrast to the keystroke gestures, the scratch-out gesture requires that you have ink on the writing pad. Scratch-out allows you to erase ink you just wrote before it leaves the writing pad. A scratch-out must be at least 2.5 lines, shaped like a flat Z, that intersect the ink you want to erase. Scratch-out works more consistently if you don't try to cover the ink you want to erase with the scratch-out mark. Instead, go back and forth over the same line in a very horizontal motion. Whatever ink intersects that line should disappear. Both examples in Table 2-3 can result in a scratch-out, but the upper one will produce more reliable results.

Table 2-3 Make your scratch-out back and forth over the same spot instead of trying to cover the entire item.

Scratch Out Gesture

Better Scratch Out

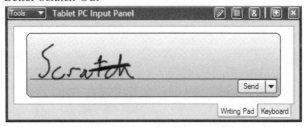

Worse Scratch Out

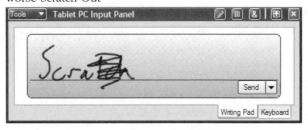

Try This   Open a blank document in your favorite e-mail program, and try writing a quick letter to a friend using Input Panel. Use the pen to tap your way through creating a new message and entering his or her e-mail address. Use the Input Panel keyboard to tap in your e-mail address in the CC box. Write a sentence using the writing pad with text preview off, and correct it in the message. Next write a sentence with text preview on, and make your corrections in the text preview pane. Try mixtures of the different input methods and see which system works best for you and in what contexts.

Write Anywhere

The Input Panel writing pad works well for a few sentences, but writing on the same line over and over is not how we really handwrite messages. The Write Anywhere feature essentially turns most of the tablet screen into a transparent writing pad. This is a powerful feature, but it can be confusing because it appears that you're writing directly on a document, as you can with Windows Journal and Microsoft Office XP with the Office XP Pack for Tablet PC. You're not. Write Anywhere is a version of the Input Panel writing pad and is still a method for text entry when the keyboard is not accessible or convenient.

Turning On Write Anywhere

To use Write Anywhere, first open the document in which you want to place text. Next open Input Panel, and tap the **Write Anywhere** button on the title bar. The Write Anywhere button has an image of a pen on it. If the Write Anywhere button is not visible, tap the Tools menu on Input Panel and tap Options to display the Options dialog box. On the Write Anywhere tab, check the Show The Turn On Write Anywhere Button On The Title Bar check box and tap OK.

When you tap the Write Anywhere button, a Write Anywhere information dialog box appears. Tap OK, and the Write Anywhere boundaries appear on the screen as shown in Figure 2-13, where Write Anywhere is open on top of a new message in Microsoft Outlook Express.

There are three important items to note in this figure:

- The writing area does not extend to the edges of the screen. Only handwriting drawn within the bounded area is translated to text. Pen actions outside the area are interpreted as mouse commands. This division keeps menus, the taskbar, and open and close boxes free of the writing area for easy access. You can still control the mouse under the transparent writing area, but it's a bit trickier.

- Input Panel should be docked and hidden at the bottom of the screen. This is not required, but it's a good way to start out when using Write Anywhere. If the writing pad of Input Panel is visible under the Write Anywhere transparency and you write over the actual Input Panel writing pad, the writing pad overrides Write Anywhere. The result can be confusing and is best avoided until you get comfortable with Write Anywhere. Either hiding or docking Input Panel will avoid the problem. I prefer to do both.

■ The cursor is ready at the point in the document where the text should go. It doesn't matter where on the writing area you write, the text will insert at the cursor in the order you wrote it. To place the cursor in a different position, tap that point on the screen. If you are placing the cursor somewhere under the writing area transparency, it should be a firm tap you hold for a moment so that the system knows it's a tap (mouse action) and not a period (handwriting).

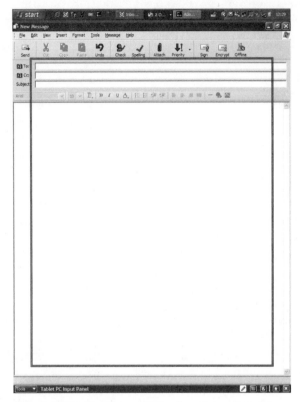

Figure 2-13   To turn on Write Anywhere, first open a document, open Input Panel, and then tap the Write Anywhere button. It helps if you hide or dock Input Panel while using Write Anywhere.

Using Write Anywhere

Once the writing area transparency is open and the cursor is in place, you can begin writing. As shown in Figure 2-14, wherever you start writing, a black line appears to help you write horizontally across the screen. You do not need to write on the line, but the recognition is better if your handwriting does not wander all over the screen. As with the writing pad on Input Panel, there's an adjustable delay before the ink disappears and the text appears in the document.

Figure 2-14   Tap once to place the cursor where you want text to go, and then start writing anywhere on the writing area transparency.

When you're using the Input Panel writing pad, you must specify each Enter, extra Space, and Tab. If you do not, the system will put all your text together no matter how you organize it on the screen. You can send these commands using the same gestures as with the writing pad, but the entire writing area transparency must be clear of ink. Because the ink tends to persist longer in Write Anywhere, this isn't always convenient. Another method is to open the quick keys pad from the Input Panel title bar while Write Anywhere is still open. You can tap an Enter, Tab, or other key on the quick keys pad without waiting for the ink to disappear; however, as soon as you tap a key all the ink currently in the writing area will be immediately converted to text. Figure 2-15 and Figure 2-16 show how the system would ignore text organization (new lines, tabs, and so on) and how it could be corrected.

> **Tip**   Write Anywhere also understands the scratch-out gesture to remove ink before it is converted to text.

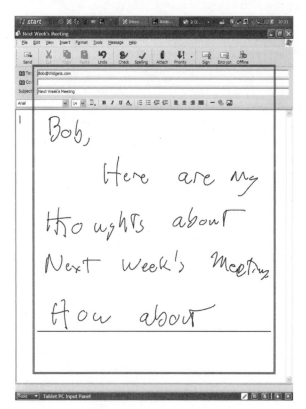

Figure 2-15   Write Anywhere allows you to write freely over the screen, but it does not interpret the organization of your text. Figure 2-16 shows how this text is interpreted.

Selecting an entire paragraph with Write Anywhere open is simple if you start the selection on the edge of the screen, outside the writing area. Press down with the pen at the beginning of the selection, and drag the pen over the text you want selected. To select text underneath the transparency, press and hold on a point under the writing transparency. The transparency temporarily vanishes and remains absent as long as you keep holding. Without lifting the pen, you may now drag the pen over the text you want selected. As soon as you lift the pen the transparency reappears, but the text remains selected. You must either disable the Press And Hold For Right-Click option or set a long pause before the shortcut menu appears for this to work; otherwise, you'll get a shortcut menu instead of a selection. If you use the Press And Hold For Right-Click option, it's usually easier to close Write Anywhere for a moment, select the text you want, open Write Anywhere again, and continue. Because the writing transparency opens and closes instantly, this hardly disturbs your work.

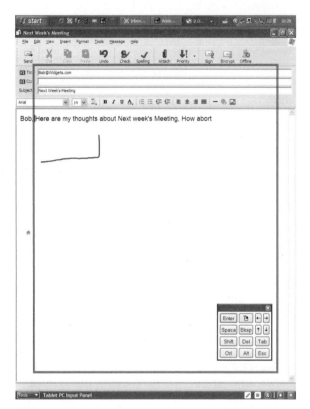

Figure 2-16   You may edit and correct text by using gestures, such as the Enter gesture shown here, by tapping keys on the quick key pad, or even by switching to the Input Panel on-screen keyboard while Write Anywhere is open.

When you reach the bottom of the writing area, you may continue writing at the top in the empty space, as shown in Figure 2-17. The text will enter your document in the same order you wrote it, regardless of where you wrote it or what is below the transparency. The text at the top of Figure 2-17 was written last and will appear at the end of the sentence.

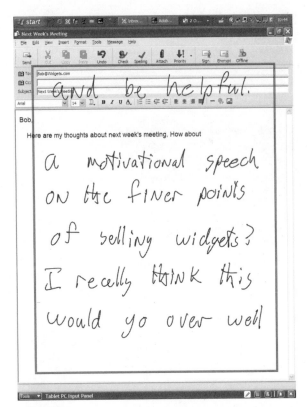

Figure 2-17 Text will be entered into your document in the same order you wrote it, regardless of where you wrote it or what is below the transparency.

Write Anywhere is a tool you will probably either love or hate. If you use Write Anywhere regularly, here are a few tips to keep things running smoothly:

■ Hide or dock Input Panel while Write Anywhere is open. If your pen enters the Input Panel window, it will interrupt your writing.

■ Tear off the quick keys pad from Input Panel so that it is available as you write. Be careful not to write on top of the quick keys pad, as the keys will respond and interrupt your writing. See "Setting Input Panel Options" later in this chapter for information on how to add the Quick Keys button on the Input Panel title bar, which allows you to tear off the quick keys pad.

- If the writing transparency is free of ink, a gesture is even faster than tapping a key on the quick keys pad.

- Remember to tap or gesture an Enter command at the end of each paragraph.

- Adjust the speed of the automatic insert so that it converts the ink as fast as possible without disturbing your writing. Write Anywhere is a drag if you must wait for the ink to disappear.

- Closing the Write Anywhere transparency will immediately convert the ink into text and send it to the cursor, similar to the Send button on the writing pad.

- Switching to a different program while there is still ink in Write Anywhere will cause that ink to appear in the new program or be lost entirely.

Try This   Open and tear off the quick keys pad and symbols pad from Input Panel, and then hide Input Panel. Next open a blank e-mail message, and try entering all the information using Write Anywhere. If possible, write a couple of paragraphs so that you can experiment with correction and editing.

Speech Input

Input Panel has speech input capabilities, which allows both dictation, in which your spoken words are converted to text, and voice commands, in which your words control menus and on-screen buttons and can switch between programs. The dictation function works similarly to the on-screen keyboard and writing pad. Place the cursor where you want the text to go, activate the dictation mode, and start speaking. After a short delay, the text appears in your document where you can correct and edit it. If the text preview pane is open, the converted text appears in the window and will be inserted in your document after you tap Send Text. The voice command function is a bit different and is discussed separately later in this section. The speech input controls appear in the speech bar below the Input Panel title bar, as shown in Figure 2-18.

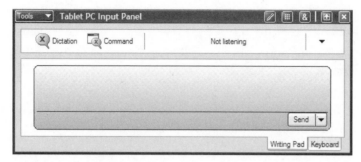

Figure 2-18   The speech bar appears below the Input Panel title bar and shows whether the speech recognizer is listening for dictation or voice commands or is not listening at all.

Hardware Considerations

For speech input to work even passably well, you need a boom microphone on a headset. Make sure you get one that is designed for use on a personal computer so that it has separate plugs for the headphones and the microphone. Two other features worth the investment are a noise-canceling microphone, which reduces interference from noise in the room, and a microphone on/off switch mounted on the wire running to the computer, which lets you easily prevent accidental voice input when you answer the phone or speak to someone else in the room. At the time of this writing, Radio Shack sold a comfortable microphone with all of these features for about $20.

> **Tip**   If the microphone jacks are in an annoying location on your tablet in portrait orientation, try using the secondary portrait orientation.

Training the System

Before you can input a single word to the tablet, you must train the system to learn your personal speech patterns. Unlike handwriting recognition, which only learns your vocabulary and not your handwriting, speech recognition actually learns how you speak and continues to improve over time. The more time you spend teaching the system the better it will be, but the initial training is required. The information is stored with your login profile, so you must log in as the same user each time when you use speech input.

How Speech Recognition Works

In many ways speech recognition is more complex than handwriting recognition because there is an even greater variety in how we speak as there is in how we write. When the speech recognition system tries to understand you it does something called pattern matching. It measures the speed, phonetics, pitch, spacing, punctuation, accent, and other aspects of your spoken words and compares them with samples in its database. As you train the speech recognition system, it narrows down the list of patterns it uses to include only the ones that closely match how you speak. This is why speech training is so important to get good results from speech input on your tablet. Without training the system, someone with a Midwest United States accent may see a speech recognition accuracy of over 95%, but the average American will get about 88% accuracy. Many native New Yorkers, Georgians, or anyone else with a stronger regional accent may see results that are much lower. With enough training of the system—and practice speaking without using "ums," "uhs," and excessive inflection—most people can get accuracies of 98%.

To open the speech bar on Input Panel, check Speech on the Input Panel Tools menu. The first time you do this, the mandatory Speech Training Wizard opens and guides you through adjusting your microphone and practicing speech input. The tutorial is very clear, but it takes 10 to 20 minutes to complete, so make sure you have at least half an hour for the wizard and trying speech out. Make sure the microphone is comfortable before you begin because changing the position of the microphone later could affect the quality of the voice recognition. After you have been guided through the microphone adjustment, you will read several paragraphs aloud. The words will be highlighted as they are recognized by the system, as shown in Figure 2-19. The highlighting will lag behind what you are actually reading. This is normal. If the highlighting stops, however, you must go back and start reading again beginning at the first un-highlighted word. Speak normally, but without much inflection, for the best results. The text of the first speech training discusses ways to improve the quality of speech recognition and often feels more like a sales pitch than helpful information. A more interesting list of items to read is available when performing further training. Speech recognition uses the same dictionary as handwriting recognition, so it learns your vocabulary as well as your voice.

Caution   Don't let friends try out the speech function on your login profile. The system will add their voice characteristics to your profile, resulting in degraded speech recognition for you. Create a guest login profile, and let them try speech that way.

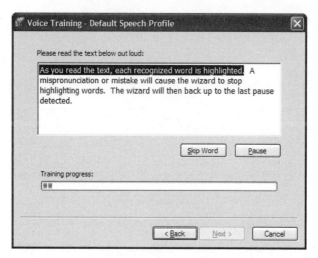

Figure 2-19   When you first open speech input, you enter a required speech training session. Optional additional sessions improve the recognition.

Tip   Position the microphone close enough to your lips so that if you pucker them in a kissing motion, you can just barely touch it. Most microphones work better if they are slightly below your lips rather than right in front of them.

Dictation

Once you complete at least the first voice training, you can input text using speech. Open a document and place the cursor where you want to input text. Next open Input Panel and make the speech bar visible. Once you tap the Dictation button, the system will show that it is listening, and everything you say, or something resembling what you say, will appear in your document. If the text preview pane is open, the text will appear there instead. Text that has been heard and is being converted appears as highlighted dots. There's no need to wait for the dots to disappear before you continue speaking. The memory buffer holding the text is quite large, and unless you speak very quickly and never take a breath it will eventually catch up. As you speak, voice bars appear on Input Panel showing the strength and variation in your voice and indicating whether your speech is too loud, soft, or fast for optimal recognition. Figure 2-20 shows some sample dictation.

Tip Turn off your microphone between inputs to prevent accidental text input. If you don't have a switch on your microphone, tap the Dictation button a second time to turn it off or say "microphone," and it will turn off.

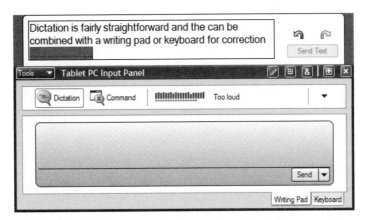

Figure 2-20   Dictation converts your speech and inserts it in the document or text preview pane. The speech bar provides feedback on the quality of the voice input.

Dictation Control Commands

There are several words which may or may not be converted directly into text depending on when and how you say them. For example, if the word "microphone" is said as part of a sentence, it will be converted to text, but if said as a single word, it will turn off the microphone. Similarly, "voice command" said as part of a sentence will appear as text, but said alone, it will switch speech input to voice command mode. Two other crucial commands you can use within dictation mode are "new paragraph," which is the equivalent of the Enter key, and "new line," which is the equivalent of Shift+Enter on your keyboard.

Spelling Out Words

If you want to spell out a word, say "spell it" and then immediately begin spelling the word. The letters will appear as you say them until you pause, at which point the system will revert to normal dictation. There is a second option called spelling mode that differs only in execution. If you say "spelling mode," you must pause before spelling the word. When you start speaking again, the word is spelled out, and when you stop, the system returns to normal dictation. If you want to select a word that has already been converted to text, you can say "spell that." "Spell that" selects whatever word is touching the cursor at that moment and lets you replace it by spelling it out. This is handy if you see a word translated incorrectly and you think the problem is that it is not in the dictionary rather than it was simply misunderstood.

Saying Punctuation, Numbers, and Symbols

You must say all punctuation as you go, so the sentence "He said: 'With this device, I can rule the world!'" would be spoken "He said colon quote with this device comma I can rule the world exclamation point quote." This system works well except for the odd sentence like: "That's my final offer, period!" which comes out "That's my final offer, . !" In these cases, the best thing to do is use the "spell it" command and spell out the word or correct it later. The system also automatically adds a space after a comma or a period and capitalizes the first word of a new sentence.

Numbers follow some special rules. The numbers zero through twenty will be spelled out. Numbers higher than that will appear as numeric values. If you want a number less than 21 written numerically, say "force num" and then the number. You do not need to spell out very large numbers, but you do need to say "point" or "decimal" for the decimal place. The speech "One million two hundred thirty-five thousand and thirteen point five" will appear as "1,235,013.5."

Most symbols can simply be spoken, and they will appear correctly. The beginning of a Web address is said "http colon slash slash." Some symbols have special ways of being said that help you get exactly what you want. The dollar sign symbol ($) is best said "dollarsign" as if it were one word. Saying "dollar…sign," with an exaggerated pause, will result in words "dollar sign." Table 2-5 lists some common symbols and how to say them:

Table 2-4   How to dictate some common symbols.

@	"at sign"	#	"pound sign"	$	"dollar sign"
^	"carat"	&	"ampersand'	%	"percent sign"
*	"asterisk"	--	"dash"	_	"underscore"
[	"open bracket"	(	"open parenthesis"	<	"less than"
]	"close bracket"	)	"close parenthesis"	>	"greater than"

Voice Commands

If you pause for a moment in dictation mode and say "voice command," the system will switch to voice command mode. Voice commands have two main functions: to correct the text you input through speech and to control the tablet without a pen or a mouse.

Making Corrections

You may correct converted text with voice command, as well as using Write Anywhere, the writing pad, or the Input Panel keyboard. Voice command lets you perform the Input Panel correction functions and provides some additional capabilities. Figure 2-21 shows the sentence "The voice command mode allows you to make changes using nothing but your voice" with an obvious error. While in voice command mode, saying "select Lloyd's" would select the incorrect text. Saying "correct Lloyd's" both selects the text and opens the alternate word list as shown in Figure 2-22. To replace the text with an alternate word off the list, say "select" and the number on the list of the correct word. To delete or respeak the text, read the name of the desired command aloud. Saying "unselect that" would cancel the selection. Voice command also allows you to select all visible text, select after certain words in the text, select text beginning at one word and ending on another, and insert the cursor before or after a specific word. Once you have made a selection, you can also change capitalization in the sentence with your voice.

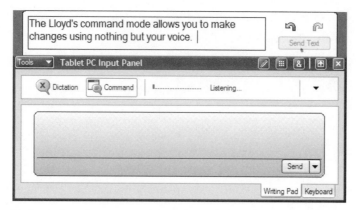

Figure 2-21   Saying or tapping "voice command" will switch you to voice command mode.

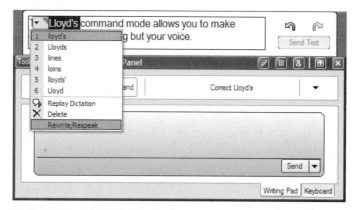

Figure 2-22   Voice command allows you to select, or select and correct text, in a single step. Input Panel displays the command it heard as it carries out the action.

What Can I Say?

Voice command does much more than give you verbal control of Input Panel. With voice command, you can open and close files, switch between applications, access the Start menu, navigate a document, and more. There are too many commands to describe them all here. To see all the commands available by voice say "What can I say?" while in voice command mode and a list similar to the one in Figure 2-23 appears. What Can I Say is context-sensitive, so the exact content of the list depends on which application you are in and even what you are doing in that application. This feature is invaluable if you use voice for anything more than dictation.

Tip   When you control a program with speech, every menu command is available even if it is not on the What Can I Say list. To control menus with speech, say the name of the menu and then the full name of the command. To see print preview, the voice command would be "File...Print Preview." If the menu doesn't show all the options right away, just pause longer after saying the menu name, and the rest of the menu will appear.

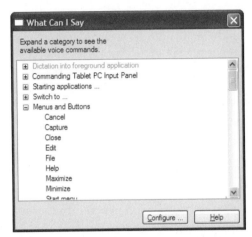

Figure 2-23   What Can I Say is a context-sensitive list of all the commands available in a given situation.

Speech Bar

The speech bar has its own options menu, shown in Figure 2-24, providing access to What Can I Say, speech help, and several speech input settings. If you're having speech recognition problems, the Microphone Adjustment option is quick and can help, especially if you are in a different room than you normally use for speech input. The Voice Training option is very helpful, but each session takes fifteen to twenty minutes. If you like speech input, it's worth your time to go through several of these sessions. You'll get the time back in the form of fewer corrections later on.

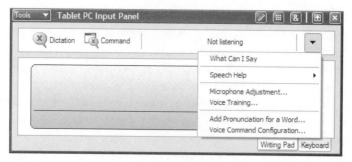

Figure 2-24   What Can I Say, microphone settings, voice training, and custom word pronunciation are available on the speech bar.

The speech recognizer understands the pronunciations of words based on spelling and grammar rules. Sometimes what it thinks the word should sound like does not match the real word very well, especially for unusual words you added to the dictionary. You have some control over this. Choosing the Add Pronunciation For A Word option opens the window shown in Figure 2-25, containing words you added. After selecting a word, you will hear the speech recognizer's top choice for the pronunciation. If it isn't correct, there is an option to record the correct pronunciation. The Record Pronunciation function is a bit misleading in that it does not record your pronunciation and associate it with the word. Instead, Record Pronunciation listens to what you say and matches your pronunciation to its list of possible pronunciations based on spelling and grammar rules. If one of its alternate pronunciations is close to yours, the association is changed and the word will probably be recognized correctly in the future. If your pronunciation doesn't match one of the alternates, then nothing happens. In my case, the correct pronunciation of Hayabasa (Hi-ya-ba-sa) doesn't match any alternate, so if I say it during dictation it always converts as "high above the." If I mispronounce it to match the way the recognizer thinks it should be said (Hi-yab-a-sa), it converts it to text correctly every time.

If you find it annoying to keep switching between dictation and voice command mode, you can make groups of voice commands available in dictation mode. The benefit is you don't have to switch modes to select and edit words. The downside is your dictation may be misunderstood as a command. To add commands to dictation mode, select Voice Command Configuration, select Working With Text, as shown in Figure 2-26, and tap Details. Check only the groups of commands you want, and check the Enable During Dictation check box.

Figure 2-25   Adding a pronunciation will sometimes fix recognition errors on words you add to the dictionary.

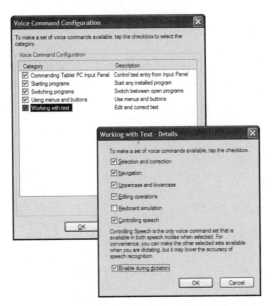

Figure 2-26   You can enable many of the voice commands so that they are available during dictation.

Other Speech Tips

Here are a few more tips to get the most out of speech input:

■ Often a combination of speech, writing, and pen in place of the mouse works best for maximum productivity.

- Different room acoustics, low-level background noise, and even your having a cold can interfere with speech recognition.

- If you hide Input Panel, the speech bar is still visible.

- Double check the choice of homonyms such as "there," "their," and "they're".

- If you're trying to control an application with speech and it isn't working, it probably isn't in the foreground. Tap the title bar of the application window to ensure it is the foremost application.

- If you regularly use speech input in a variety of noise environments, you can create separate speech profiles for each one using the Speech control panel. This will improve recognition overall, but requires training each profile separately in the appropriate environment.

Try This   Even for a good typist, retyping a document can be tedious. Reading it and having Input Panel do the typing is much more fun and usually works pretty well. Find a printed document that you would like a copy of on your computer. Open a blank word processor document, place the cursor, and activate speech input in dictation mode. Read all the paragraphs, saying "new paragraph" when needed, without correcting any mistakes. Next switch to voice command mode, and save the document with voice commands, switching to dictation briefly to give it a name. Finally, try correcting the recognition mistakes with a combination of voice commands, pen taps, and writing pad inputs.

Setting Input Panel Options

Customizing Input Panel so that it matches your needs is essential for long-term enjoyment of your tablet. As with the pen settings, the default settings are geared toward the complete beginner. Once you gain experience using the various Input Panel functions, using more advanced settings will increase the speed and utility of Input Panel. You can open the Input Panel options by tapping the Tools menu in Input Panel and tapping Options.

Improving Writing Speed

If you fill the writing pad with ink faster than the tablet takes it away, you have two options. As shown in Figure 2-27, the writing pad options allow for a two-line writing pad and a shorter delay before the ink is converted to text. The two-line pad allows you to fill one line with ink and then continue on the second. By the time the second line is full, the first line should be empty, and you continue writing up there. This back and forth actually flows quite naturally after a few tries and works quite well. The only disadvantage is you must write a bit smaller and with your letters closer together, or you must resize Input Panel to take up more of the screen. A shorter insertion time has a similar effect except that the ink is disappearing off the beginning of the line as you are writing on the end. The setting can actually get so fast that the ink disappears before you even finish the word! Try various combinations of both settings until you can both write comfortably and see your ink for at least a moment before it disappears, never waiting more than half a second or so for a place to write.

Figure 2-27 A two-line writing pad and a shorter delay before insertion allow you to write continuously on the writing pad without waiting for the screen to clear of ink.

Write Anywhere has a separate setting for automatic insertion time. Since Write Anywhere is already a several-line writing pad, the delay can be much longer. In fact, it is usually helpful to have extra time in Write Anywhere to scratch out mistakes. Still, the delay should be short enough so that you are never waiting for a place to write. The setting for the Write Anywhere insertion time is on the Write Anywhere tab in the Input Panel options.

> **Note**   You can turn off automatic insertion altogether, so you must tap the Send button to clear the ink. This setting only applies to text. Gestures are immediately interpreted and cleared from the writing pad.

Better Tool Access and Configuration

There are several settings that allow you to customize your workspace for maximum utility.

- **Title Bar Buttons**   The Advanced tab of Input Panel options lets you put quick-access buttons on the Input Panel title bar for opening the quick keys pad, the symbols pad, and hiding or showing Input Panel. As mentioned earlier, after tapping the button for the quick keys pad or symbols pad you may make a one-key tap or tear off the pad into a floating palette. The title bar button to turn Write Anywhere on and off is activated on the Write Anywhere tab.

- **Input Panel Autohide**   On the Advanced tab, you can set an undocked Input Panel to automatically minimize to a title bar after a period of inactivity, so long as it is undocked. The full Input Panel reappears as soon as your pen comes near the title bar. This is a great feature if you like an undocked Input Panel. Making the delay very short, one second or less, has the effect of having Input Panel appear the moment you need it and roll up into an unobtrusive title bar a moment after you are done. Floating palettes and the speech bar will not disappear with autohide.

- **Automatic Text Preview with Speech**   When you dictate, Input Panel can check and see whether the application you are dictating into supports alternate words. If it does, the text goes directly to the application; if it does not, the text preview pane opens automatically, and the text appears there instead. This option is activated on the Speech tab.

- **Pen Width and Color**   The pen width and ink color for both the writing pad and Write Anywhere are configured on the Write Anywhere tab in the Input Panel options. The setting is purely one of personal preference and can be different for the two writing situations.

> **Tip**   Set the Write Anywhere ink color to something not commonly used by Windows and visible over both light and dark backgrounds. I use a darkish magenta. This lets you see the ink on the writing transparency regardless of what image is beneath it.

■ **Writing Tools**   You have already seen how the quick keys pad can appear both as a floating palette and in the writing pad window. The Writing Tools tab sets whether the quick keys appear on the writing pad as well and whether they appear on the right or the left. The Writing Tools tab also lets you use a character recognizer for text input using either the Palm Pilot Graffiti or Pocket PC letter system.

Why Not Use the Character Recognizer

The Writing Tools tab in Input Panel options allows you to enable the character recognizer for Input Panel and convert shorthand symbols, like those used on a Palm Pilot or Pocket PC, into typed text. As shown in Figure 2-28, the character recognizer takes up a lot of space, which makes the writing pad less useful. One interesting benefit of the character recognizer is that it can correct text and replace the quick keys pad for typing Enter, Tab, Space, and Backspace keys. If you do use the character recognizer, a character reference appears in the Input Panel Help files. Somewhat akin to the difference between hunt-and-peck and touch typing, after a little practice, using your own handwriting will always be faster and more efficient than using shorthand symbols.

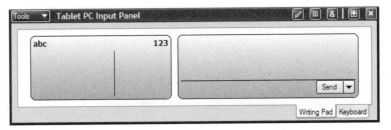

Figure 2-28   The character recognizer displayed on the left of Input Panel.

Send as Text vs. Send as Ink

As flexible and useful as Input Panel is, we have been looking at it as a bridge between old and new technology. It is a method of translating from a medium humans understand, handwriting or speech, to a medium the computer can manipulate, standardized characters. Once the ink vanishes off Input Panel and converts it to text, it is lost.

Input Panel can send the actual pen strokes, or ink, from the writing pad, as well as the list of possible meanings, to the application. Some applications can't accept this kind of data, but many can. Exactly how the ink will appear in the document and to what extent you can edit it varies; in some the pen strokes and the alternate word list are available, and in others the ink is converted into a static, un-editable image.

To send ink off the writing pad as ink, place the cursor in the document where you want the ink to appear and then tap the down arrow to the right of the Send button on Input Panel. If the Send As Ink option is available, the application you chose will accept the ink. Select Send As Ink, and whatever you write will appear in the document as ink. Figure 2-29 shows an example with Word 2002. We will explore sending ink directly to applications further in Chapter 6. In the next three chapters, we will look at Windows Journal, in which the ink goes directly into the application without the need for Input Panel at all.

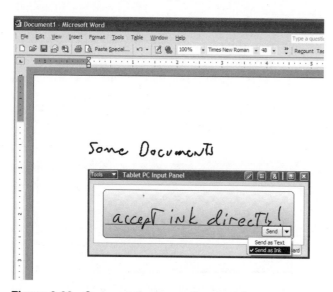

Figure 2-29 Some applications will accept the pen strokes off the writing pad as ink as well as text.

Key Points

- Input Panel is used primarily for text input when a standard keyboard is not available or convenient.

- Input Panel works with all applications that run under Windows XP.

- Maximum productivity and satisfaction come from using the various input methods on Input Panel in conjunction with a standard keyboard. Select the proper tool for a given task.

- The handwriting recognizer doesn't learn your handwriting, but following some simple guidelines will improve recognition accuracy.

- The handwriting recognizer does learn your vocabulary, and adding words to the dictionary is critical for improved handwriting recognition.

- The speech recognizer learns both your speech pattern and your vocabulary. Training the system and adding words to the dictionary are both important.

- Some applications allow text correction in the final document. For the rest, use the text preview pane.

- Time spent customizing Input Panel to meet your work preferences is time well spent.

- Input Panel is most often used to convert your handwriting to text, but it can send original pen strokes (ink) to an application as well.

3

Getting Started with Windows Journal

Windows Journal is the "killer application" on your new tablet. It's an excellent example of good software design: simple and intuitive enough to start using with minimum instruction, yet packed with powerful features awaiting your discovery. On the surface, Windows Journal works like a pad of paper. To take notes, simply place your pen on the screen and start writing. In fact, a great deal of design effort went into making Journal behave as much like real paper as possible. If you start thinking about Journal as a pad of paper, you'll be off to a great start.

In this and upcoming chapters, you'll discover some of the capabilities of Journal. For example, you'll learn how your pen can write in several colors, work as a highlighter, and how it can erase. You'll learn how to add and remove space in your notes, cut and paste your handwriting, and format your handwriting into bold and italics. You'll also learn how to search your handwritten notes for specific words and how to import documents from programs like Microsoft Word and mark them up with pen and highlighter as easily as if they had been printed out. These latent features are the real power of Journal. You can use Journal at whatever level of sophistication meets your needs in a given situation. If you're reading this book, you probably want to find out all the cool features of Journal, so let's dive in.

Just Start Writing

The best way to get going with Journal is to take a few moments to just start writing and exploring the user interface. Figure 3-1 shows the default Journal page. Try out the different pens, highlighters, and erasers in the Pen toolbar to get a feel for them. To switch between them, tap the down arrow to the right of the tool and select the particular pen, highlighter, or eraser you want. Most people have a definite "Oooh-Aaah" reaction the first time they use the chisel tip pen. It makes everyone's handwriting look better, even mine.

Figure 3-1   These are the major components of Journal.

As shown in the figure, the major components of Journal are as follows:

- **Note body**   This is your digital paper. Write or draw here to your heart's content. When you fill a page, tap the New Page button in the lower right corner to start a new page.

- **Note title**   When you first save the note, the default filename will be the note title converted to text, although you can change the name to anything you want before you save. When you list all your notes, you will see the actual ink of this title as well as the filename. See "Saving and Opening Notes" later in this chapter for more information.

- **File buttons** These are the familiar buttons for new and save, as well as buttons for importing documents into Journal and searching notes, discussed in Chapter 5. The button with the folder icon opens a list of recent notes. The note list can be used to open notes, but it is a little different than a standard open function. See "Saving and Opening Notes" later in this chapter for more information.

- **Editing buttons** Cut, copy, paste, undo, and redo buttons are similar to what you find in Word. There is also a view setting allowing you to zoom in and out on a note.

- **Pen tools** These tools control the behavior of your pen and are described in "Using Pens and Highlighters" and "Using Erasers" later in this chapter. Pen tools include Pen, Highlighter, Eraser, Selection Tool, Insert/Remove Space, and Flag.

- **New Page, Next, and Previous** The double arrow buttons will scroll up or down one page. If you are on the last page of the note and scroll down one page, a new blank page is appended to the note.

Using Pens and Highlighters

The default settings provide five pens of various colors, tip types, and tip sizes. Once you have seen what these pens can do, you can customize the pen palette as you need to for different uses. Do you need a very fine red point for editing documents? An extra fine black point for detailed drawing? A four mm purple chisel marker for calligraphy? Open the Pen And Highlighter Settings dialog box by selecting Pen Settings from the bottom of the pen menu, as shown in Figure 3-2.

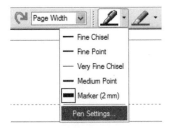

Figure 3-2 Try out different pen types and build a custom palette that meets your needs.

In the Pen And Highlighter Settings dialog box, shown in Figure 3-3, select the pen you want to change. Next select the color, thickness, and tip style you want for the new pen. A point tip is similar to a ballpoint or rollerball pen. A chisel is similar to a fountain pen. Try some wild colors and pen sizes while you're at it.

Figure 3-3   Use the Pen And Highlighter Settings dialog box to modify your pen settings.

> **Tip**   Create a color code system for your notes and make a pen for each color. For example, your notes could be in black, "to do" items in red, and ideas in purple. When you review your notes it's easy to pick out each type of information. You can also create a similar system with highlighters.

Highlighters are selected and used just like pens, except that the ink is partially transparent and the tips are wider. The five highlighter colors, thicknesses, and tips can be customized as well. Highlighter colors will also mix, so if you highlight an area with yellow and then again with blue, wherever the colors overlap the highlight will be green. Going over an area with the same color several times, however, will not make it any darker.

Pressure Sensitivity

Checking the Pressure Sensitivity check box in the Pen And Highlighter Settings dialog box creates a pen or highlighter that responds to pressure—the harder you press, the wider the ink. The feature really shows with chisel tip pens and markers, as you can see in Figure 3-4. Unfortunately, not all tablet digitizer systems support pressure sensitivity. The pressure sensitivity option will appear whether or not your tablet hardware supports it. If it pressure sensitivity doesn't seem to work, it's probably not available on your tablet.

Figure 3-4   Here's an example of what can be done with a pressure-sensitive chisel tip

Try This   To get a feel for how the ink you create in Journal differs from the lines you might make in a paint program like Microsoft Paint, open them both and draw a curved line. Now zoom in on each line and compare the two. The Journal line will be equally smooth at any zoom setting. The Paint line will get more and more grainy, or *pixilated*, as you zoom in. This is because Journal records your ink strokes as complex equations, called Bezier curves, rather than as dots on the screen. The result is a line that is smoothed as you write it and is equally clear no matter how you resize it. This same technology is used by artists operating high-end computer illustration software. The Bezier curve also stores the direction the line was drawn, which provides key information for handwriting recognition.

Using Erasers

The eraser tool is used just like a pen: select a small, medium, or large eraser tip and press down as you erase. The eraser cursor is square, but if you cut an ink stroke with the eraser, the trimmed ends will appear rounded or chiseled depending on the pen used to draw the stroke. Looking closely at the left-hand image in Figure 3-5 you can see how the end of the line is rounded even though it was cut with a square eraser. The stroke eraser, the fourth eraser type, is a "smart eraser" and works differently from the other three. The right-hand image shown in Figure 3-5 was tapped in exactly the same spot as the left-hand image but it was done using the stroke eraser. Because I drew the circle of the bug's head as a single pen stroke, the stroke eraser removed the entire thing. The stroke eraser allows you to remove large areas of ink quickly, and you can selectively remove ink strokes that cross other ink strokes. In the right-hand image of Figure 3-5, the antennae remained intact even though they crossed over the circle of the bug's head. Once you get used to it, you'll probably use the stroke eraser most of the time.

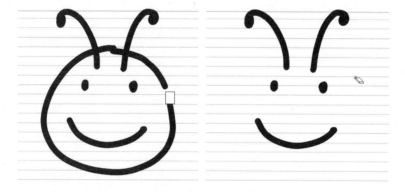

Figure 3-5   A normal eraser is used on the left and a stroke eraser is used on the right. The stroke eraser removes entire ink strokes at once.

> **Tip**   The stroke eraser is a great way to erase highlighting but leave the underlying ink untouched.

Some tablet pens have a feature that you almost have to see to believe. These pens have a plastic "eraser" on the top. This eraser is really a button. If you flip the pen over and press down with the eraser as you move it, Journal automatically switches to the eraser tool! When you flip it back, the pen will revert to whatever tool you had selected previously. You can't get much more intuitive than that! Some pens have a two-position button on the pen shaft that provides the normal right-tap when you push it one way and does a quick switch to the eraser when you move it the other way. Some pens even have both quick eraser buttons. Journal also supports multiple undos, providing another great way to remove recent mistakes.

Scratch Out Gesture

Journal also supports the scratch out gesture used in Tablet PC Input Panel and Write Anywhere. The gesture is a bit harder to get right in Journal because the system must now decide if you are scratching out or simply shading in a picture. As with the other scratch out gestures, you do not need to cover the entire object for scratch out to remove the entire stroke. The scratch out in Figure 3-6 would remove the entire word "Out," similar to crossing the letters with the stroke eraser. You must, however, make the gesture aggressively, with horizontal strokes, and move back and forth at least two and one half times. The availability of the eraser, especially the stroke eraser, somewhat obviates the need for scratch out in Journal.

Figure 3-6   Journal supports the scratch out gesture.

> **Note**   The scratch out gesture must be enabled on the Other tab of the Journal Options dialog box to have an effect. If you get scratch outs when you don't want them, you can disable this feature.

Flags

Flags are a very simple but powerful feature. The Flag tool places a flag graphic in your document wherever you tap. This is a great way to mark a point in your document so you can easily find it later. When you review a list of notes, you'll see at a glance which ones contain flags. When you open a note, the Find command, discussed in Chapter 5, lets you quickly find all the flags in the note. There are five flag colors, so you can use different ones to represent different types of items. You cannot, however, limit the search to flags of a particular color. Each flag is simply a graphic, and can be moved around or resized however you wish.

Changing the View

Journal lets you zoom in and out on the page, a feature that leaves traditional paper in the dust. This is great way to touch up a hand-drawn picture or do some precise erasing. There are three ways to zoom in and out: select a new zoom setting from the Standard toolbar, select a new zoom setting from the View menu, or open and use the View toolbar, as shown in Figure 3-7. The View toolbar also gives you the Pan tool, whose icon is a small hand, which allows you to slide the paper around on the screen while you are zoomed in.

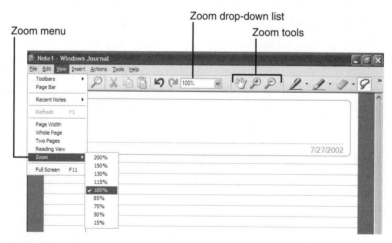

Figure 3-7   Changing the view.

Zooming in can create problems if you don't realize how it works. By default, new notes are shown with the paper sized to fit the available screen. This gives you the most screen area to write on, but it means your handwriting may end up very large or very small depending on the size and settings of your screen. If you write at your normal writing size with the zoom set at 50%, 100%, or 200%, the actual ink strokes will get progressively smaller. The pen will appear thicker when zoomed in, as well, since the width of the tip is a set number of millimeters. Figure 3-8 shows this effect, where the word written the same size on the screen will appear as three different sizes on the page. This is not a big deal if you never print your notes, but if you do print them the results can be somewhat unexpected.

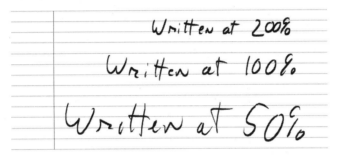

Figure 3-8   Ink drawn at different zoom settings will appear different sizes relative to the page.

Calibrating Journal Paper Size

You may have noticed how one inch on the computer screen often doesn't print as one inch on paper. Journal has a feature that corrects this so that a one-inch measurement on screen will print at exactly one inch. Even if you never print your notes, it's a good idea to make this calibration. Pen tips simulate particular sized pens and will appear smoother and more natural if the on-screen size is correct. This is especially true of the very fine and extra fine pens.

To calibrate the size of your notes, select Options on the Tools menu. On the Note Format tab, tap Display Measurements to display the Adjust Display Measurements dialog box, shown in Figure 3-9. Now take a real ruler and lay it across your screen. Adjust the slider until the inches on the screen match the inches on the ruler. Tap OK once you're done. From now on, whatever you draw at 100% zoom will print at exactly the same size.

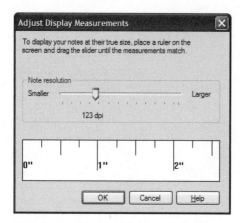

Figure 3-9   Use this slider to calibrate the paper size.

Reading View

Reading view will set the view so that you can see the entire page or part of the page based on the available screen area and the size of the ink and type you are reading. You specify reading view by selecting Reading View from the Zoom drop-down list on the Standard toolbar or by selecting Reading View from the View menu. While in reading view, pressing the Up or Down arrow keys will advance the note one entire page rather than just one line. The Spacebar also advances the note one screen or page. This is very convenient for reviewing notes and editing documents, especially if the Up and Down keys are mapped to hardware buttons or you have the page bar visible, as discussed in Chapter 5. You may still write, highlight, and erase normally in reading view. Switching the zoom to any other setting will quit reading view.

Full-Screen Mode

Similar to full-screen mode in Microsoft Internet Explorer, full-screen mode in Journal causes the Journal title bar and taskbar to disappear and Journal to fill the screen, as shown in Figure 3-10. You can toggle between full-screen mode and normal mode by selecting Full Screen on the View menu or by pressing F11 on the input panel keyboard. If you're going to work in Journal for a while and won't be switching to other applications often, full-screen mode makes the most of the available screen space and removes any distractions. You may use any zoom setting in full-screen mode, including reading view. Full-screen mode also uses separate toolbar preferences, so you can set different default toolbars.

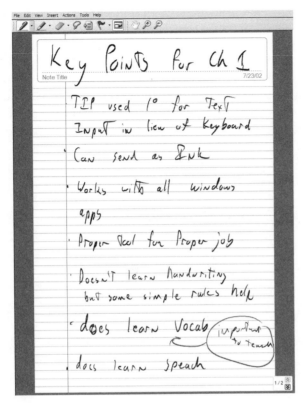

Figure 3-10   Full-screen mode makes the most of limited screen space.

Saving and Opening Notes

As mentioned earlier, the handwritten note title will be converted to text and set as the default name for your note. If there's no title, the first recognizable text appears as the default filename. If the default text is what you want as the filename, tap the Save button and the note will be saved. If the text is incorrect, you will need to correct it using Input Panel. The filename need not match the note title, but it reduces confusion if you can keep them the same. By default, your notes are saved in a new My Notes folder in your My Documents folder.

Note   The note title area only applies to the first page of a multi-page note. The note title area does not appear on subsequent pages.

Note List

You can open a note by double-tapping the actual file in your My Notes folder, but using the note list in Journal provides a lot more options. Tapping the **View Recent Notes** toolbar button in Journal opens the note list pane shown in Figure 3-11. The note list shows the ink contained in the title area of the note as well as the filename, so you can find a note either way. If there's no ink in the note title area, that column is left blank. The note list pane is also a kind of notes browser. Whatever note you select in the note list is opened in the window below, and tapping the Previous or Next buttons or pressing the Up or Down arrow key will open the next note in the list.

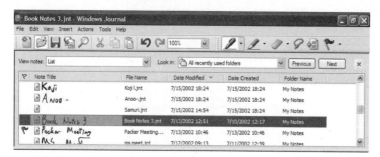

Figure 3-11   The note list pane shows you the note title in ink as well as the filename.

> **Tip**   Double-tapping a filename in the Journal notes opens it in new window. Right-tapping a filename opens a shortcut menu options for opening, moving, deleting, or sending the note.

You can also organize the note list view by folder, creation date, modification date, or show only the notes containing flags. Figure 3-12 shows notes organized by creation date, a handy feature if you can't remember what you called that note you wrote last Thursday. Tapping any column title will sort the notes by that column in descending order as well. Tapping a second time will sort them in ascending order. A red flag to the left of the note title appears if there are any flags in the document, regardless of their color. The note list is further customizable by right-tapping on any column heading. The resulting shortcut menu lets you turn on several more fields. For example, the Flags column showing the number of flags in each document, as seen in Figure 3-12, is not on by default and was added using this shortcut menu.

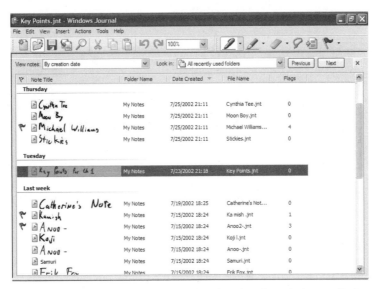

Figure 3-12   Note list offers organizational tools to help you find your notes.

> **Note**   You can customize the position of the note list, as well as number of recently used folders and note listed in the note list, using the View tab of the Journal Options dialog box. You can also set whether the list of recently used notes in the file menu appears as note titles or filenames.

Deleting Notes

Since many notes are only needed for a short time, deletion of unneeded notes is made easier by a Delete Note option on the File menu. The Delete Note command works on the note you have open or the note you have selected in the note list. This is a very handy command when you are cleaning out old notes without the use of a keyboard and don't have a hardware button for delete.

> **Tip**   You can delete the note currently selected in the note list by pressing the Delete key on Input Panel.

Adding Pages

Once you fill a page, tap the New Page/Next button in the lower right of the Journal window. If you're in the middle of a multi-page note, this button scrolls the view down one page. If you're on the last page of the note, this button adds a new page to the end of the note. You can also insert a page before the page you are viewing by selecting New Page from the Insert menu. Use this feature if you want to add a cover page before sharing a note.

> **Note**   The New Page/Next button will not create a new page if the current page is still blank.

Inserting and Removing Space on the Page

Often when writing a note, especially a list, you need to add an item between two items already on the note. With traditional paper you're out of luck, but not with Journal. To insert vertical space in between items on a note, choose the **Insert/Remove Space** tool on the Pen toolbar and bring the cursor to the point in the document that you want to expand, as shown in Figure 3-13. Next drag downward to indicate how much extra space you want, and lift the pen. All the ink below the insertion point will move downward on the page, allowing you to write in the additional space. The Insert/Remove Space tool won't split up grouped ink, so if there's ink on both sides of the insertion point it will either all move down or all stay put, depending on which side of the insertion point the majority of the ink lies. To remove space, place the Insert/Remove Space tool at the bottom of the blank space and drag upward. When you remove space, you can only remove space that's completely free of ink. The Insert/Remove Space tool won't delete ink.

> **Glossary**   *Grouped ink* is a set of several ink strokes that should stay together if they're moved throughout the document, such as all the strokes that create a single word. See "Selecting Ink" and "Grouping Ink" later in this chapter for more information.

If the ink moved down will no longer fit on the page, you'll see the Space Tool dialog box, shown in Figure 3-14, asking if you want to increase the height of the page or move the ink below the insertion onto a new page. If you increase the height, you'll have one page that is longer than all the others. This is only a problem if you plan to print the note, as one page will print differently. If you move the ink to a new page, all the ink below the insertion point will move to a new page, even if there's still room for some of the ink on the current page.

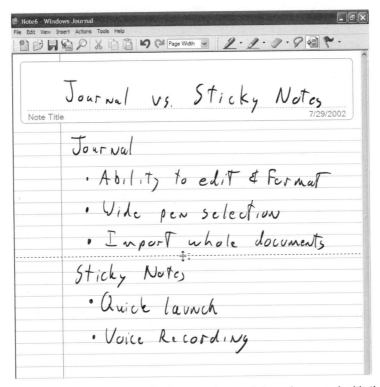

Figure 3-13 To add vertical space, tap and drag downward with the Insert/Remove Space tool.

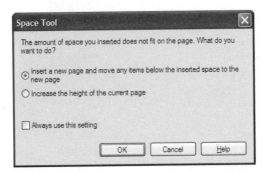

Figure 3-14 Dialog box that appears if there isn't enough space on the page when using the Insert/Remove Space tool.

> **Note**   By default, the Insert/Remove Space tool will only insert space in increments the same size as the rules on your page. If it did not, you would almost certainly end up with some extra wide or extra narrow spaces between rules. You can disable this option on the View tab of the Journal Options dialog box.

Editing Notes

If Journal did nothing more than supply a digital writing pad, it would still be useful, but it's the power to select and edit ink that makes Journal really shine. To select ink and move it to a new location, select the **Selection Tool** on the Pen toolbar and circle (or lasso, as the icon might imply) the ink you want selected. As ink is added to the selection, it appears in an outline format. Once you have all the ink selected, lift your pen. The selection is bounded by a box. To move the ink, tap and drag anywhere inside the box. Tap anywhere outside the box or switch back to a pen tool to deselect and continue writing. Figure 3-15 shows the process.

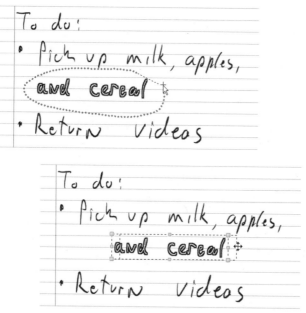

Figure 3-15   Selecting and moving ink.

Selecting usually works easily and intuitively, but sometimes the Selection Tool seems to select extra items you didn't want or won't let you select the items you do want. The key to successful editing is understanding how to select exactly the objects you want, and the key to precise selection is understanding how Journal groups the ink you put down on the page.

Selecting Ink

When you write words on a page, Journal looks at the many strokes of ink you made and groups them together based on a complex logic system. For example, take the words "ink object." The word "ink" is actually five pen strokes: the body of the i, the dot on the i, the n, the tall part of the k, and the short part of the k. Ideally, Journal will group all these strokes together so that when I select the word they all move together, and won't leave out the dot on the i or part of the k. When you select with the Selection Tool, if 50% of a group of strokes is contained by the lasso, the entire group is selected. If less than 50% is contained by the lasso, none of the group is selected. Table 3-1 shows examples of the Selection Tool attempting to select the word "ink" out of "ink object" and the results.

Table 3-1   Results of selecting objects.

Ink Object	Selected Words	Notes
	<none>	The original ink strokes
	ink	Selecting "ink"

(continued)

Table 3-1   Results of selecting objects.   *(continued)*

Ink Object	Selected Words	Notes
	ink	Selecting at least 50% of "ink"
	ink	Selecting "ink" and less than 50% of "object"
	ink object	Selecting "ink" and more than 50% of "object"

Grouping Ink

The grouping of ink strokes is done automatically as you write. If Journal groups strokes that you want to select individually, you can ungroup the strokes. To do this, select the group containing the strokes you want ungrouped and then choose Ungroup from the Actions menu. Now all the strokes are selectable individually. You can also group strokes so that they always stay together as a single object, as you might prefer with a hand-drawn map. To group ink strokes, select all the strokes you want to group and choose Group from the Actions menu. Now all the strokes will stay together if you select them in the document. If several strokes make up a word but are not recognized as such, select the strokes and choose Group As One Word instead of Group.

> **Note**   Grouping is essential for Journal to recognize your handwriting as text. If you group several words as one in an effort to keep them together, handwriting recognition will not understand those words correctly.

Resizing Ink

Whenever ink is selected, you can drag any handle on the selection box to resize it. Dragging a corner handle will change the height and width proportionally. Dragging a middle handle will distort the shape. When creating maps or diagrams, it's often easier to draw them large and then select and resize them smaller to fit better on the page, as shown in Figure 3-16.

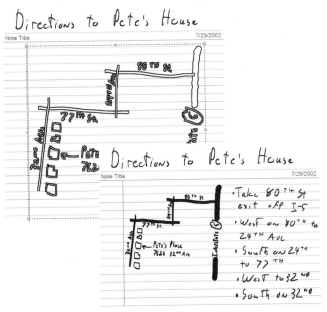

Figure 3-16   Select and resize ink to make room as necessary.

Clever Selecting

There are several selection shortcuts and tricks to make selection easier.

- **Tap to Select**   The quickest way to select a group is to choose the Selection Tool and tap anywhere on the ink you want selected. This will select the entire group. In the "ink object" example earlier in this chapter, tapping anywhere on the word "ink" selected the entire word. Tapping to select is especially useful for selecting shapes surrounding words.

> **Tip**   If you draw a box around text and it is too small, tap the box to select it without selecting the text and then increase the box size to fit more text.

- **Multiple Selections**   To select multiple objects, you can select one object, tap the Ctrl button on Input Panel (or hold the Ctrl key on a standard keyboard), and then select additional objects.

- **Crescent Selections**   You can make a crescent-shaped selection that gets only the items you want and avoids the rest. Figure 3-17 shows an example.

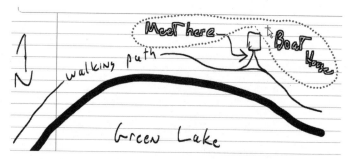

Figure 3-17   Using a crescent selection to select multiple objects.

- **Right-tap, Tap-and-hold, or Right-drag selection**   If you right-tap, tap-and-hold, or right-drag when you select, you will get a shortcut menu with several options for editing or formatting the selection. Formatting ink is discussed in Chapter 4.

Tip   You don't need to switch to the Selection Tool to select objects using right-tap, tap-and-hold, or right-drag. This lets you make selections without changing tools.

Select All and Select Page

Select All and Select Page appear in the Edit menu and serve two distinct functions. Select All will select all the objects, including ink, flags, text boxes, and images, on the *current* page, even if they're currently off the screen. Once the objects are selected, you can resize all the items or paste them onto a different page. Select Page selects all the items on a page, plus the background. After selecting a page, the options on the Edit menu change. Now you can Copy Page, Cut Page, or Delete Page. If you copy or cut the page, you can paste the entire page into a different note. A pasted page is always inserted before the page you are viewing.

Tip   There's no way to merge two notes, but you can use Select All and Select Page to paste notes together one page at a time.

Cutting Ink Strokes

You cannot select only part of a solid ink stroke, but you can cut an ink stroke in two with the Eraser tool and then select only one part. The erased area must be big enough that Journal understands you are cutting the ink rather than simply making a small correction. If after you cut a stroke the two parts remain grouped, manually ungroup them with the Ungroup command. Once separated, you can select and move each part. This is very helpful when editing a combination of text and drawings, as shown in Figure 3-18.

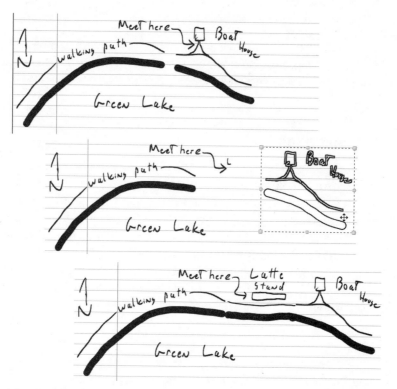

Figure 3-18 Use the Eraser tool to cut an ink stroke, ungroup if needed, and edit the ink.

Copy and Paste Ink

You can cut, copy, and paste ink objects within a note and into another note, the same way you can cut and paste text or graphics in most applications. When you paste ink into another application, Journal will paste the selection differently depending on what the application supports. Ideally, the ink itself will be pasted so that you can edit or convert it to text at a later date. If the application does not support ink, the next best option is to paste it as an image that can be resized but not edited. If neither option is available, the selected ink will be converted into text and pasted as text that may contain recognition errors. Figure 3-19 shows the result of pasting ink into Microsoft Outlook Express, where it has become a static image. For information on converting text in a Journal note to e-mail, see "Converting Selection to E-Mail" later in this chapter.

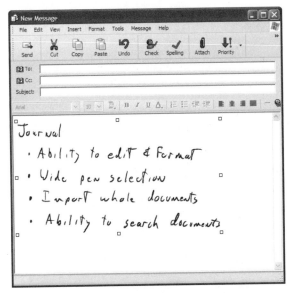

Figure 3-19   Journal will paste ink into another application as ink, a static image, or text, depending on the situation.

Tip   If you select ink, tap the Ctrl button on Input Panel or hold down the Ctrl button on a standard keyboard, and then drag the selection. A copy of the selection appears in the new location.

Converting Handwriting to Text

Every time you put ink on a page, Journal assesses the strokes to see if they might form a word. If Journal thinks the strokes do represent a word, they're grouped and the handwriting recognizer records its best guess for the word as well as several alternatives. The list of possible words is stored as part of the Journal note. The process happens in the background, so it doesn't interfere with your work, but if you choose to convert your handwriting to text, the recognition is already complete.

To access the recognized words and convert your handwriting to text, select the text you want converted and choose Convert Handwriting To Text from the Actions menu. This displays the Text Correction dialog box, shown in Figure 3-20, which is a more sophisticated version of the Input Panel text preview pane.

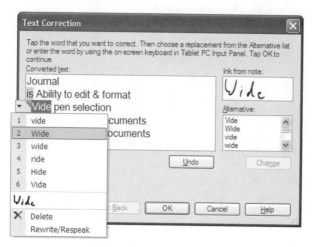

Figure 3-20   Recognition results of the Convert Handwriting To Text
command.

Correct the text in the dialog box by selecting incorrect words and either by choosing the correct word from the alternatives provided on the right or by tapping the green carat and choosing a word from the shortcut menu. The alternative list on the right of the dialog box is a little longer than the shortcut menu and offers a wider range of words. The list on the shortcut menu is the same list you would see using Input Panel. It also uses the same dictionary, so vocabulary added in Journal will appear in Input Panel as well. If you choose the Rewrite option from the shortcut menu, Input Panel will open automatically.

While the Text Correction dialog box is open you may rearrange text by dragging and dropping, and you may also add or remove line breaks. By default, a line break is entered in the converted text wherever there was a new line in the Journal note. You can remove all these automatic line breaks by tapping the Options button and unchecking Preserve Line Breaks From Notes.

When you're done, tap OK and Journal will ask if you want the converted text copied to the clipboard, preserving your original ink, or if you want the ink replaced by the converted text. This dialog box is shown in Figure 3-21.

> **Tip**   If you want the converted text put on the clipboard, choose Copy As Text from the Edit menu rather than Convert Handwriting To Text from the Actions menu. This avoids the final dialog box.

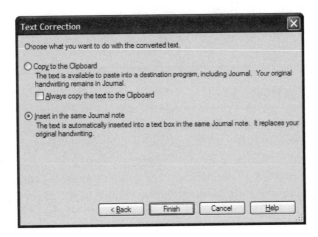

Figure 3-21   What to do with converted text.

The original handwriting doesn't need to be horizontal for recognition to work, but the order may be confused. Figure 3-22 shows multiple-orientation writing and the uncorrected converted text.

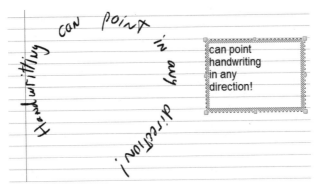

Figure 3-22   Handwriting recognition works, to an extent, in any orientation.

Converting Selection to E-Mail

If you want to convert Journal text and send it to an e-mail program, select Convert Selection To E-Mail on the Actions menu. Convert Selection To E-Mail uses the same Text Correction dialog box as Convert Handwriting To Text, but once finished, the text is inserted into the body of a new, blank e-mail message using your default e-mail program. An image of the original ink is added as an attachment as well. Convert Selection To E-Mail is a great way to delegate action items to specific people or forward a short bit of information found while reviewing your notes. If you have the Office XP Pack for Tablet PC installed, you will have additional options to convert ink to Outlook appointments, contacts, or tasks.

Fortune Telling

Here's a fun game using the convert to text function. Write your normal signature in a Journal note, select it, convert it to text and see what it says about you! My basically illegible Jeff Van West came out "Jeffy word," which seems rather appropriate for a writer. Of course, the alternate list offered "iffy word" as another interpretation, something my editors might appreciate.

Printing Notes

Printing from Journal is the same as printing from any other Windows application. Select Print from the File menu. The Options tab of the Print dialog box gives you the option to print or hide the rules on the note page and the background images. By default, the rules print but the background images do not, since they tend to interfere with readability. If you have a note where the background images are important, such as on a form, you can specify that they be printed.

Unless you write your Journal notes on an 8½-by-11-inch page, there will be a difference between the Journal note paper size and the actual paper size if you print your notes on letter-size paper. Usually the Journal note is smaller than the actual paper, in which case the note will appear at its actual size, centered in the page. If the note size is larger than the paper, it will be scaled down to fit. There is no option in Journal itself to print multiple note pages side-by-side on a single sheet of paper or to tile a note across several pages, but your printer may have options to do this.

Automatic File Recovery

File recovery is meant just as a backup system, so you should still save your notes regularly as you work. If Journal quits unexpectedly or your tablet loses power, you may be able to recover lost changes. The next time you open Journal, you'll see a list of notes, similar to Figure 3-23, with unsaved changes available for recovery, and you'll be asked if you want to open them.

If you choose No, any recovered changes will be lost. If you choose Yes, the next option will depend on whether or not you saved the note at least once before Journal quit unexpectedly. If you did, you have the option of opening the most recent version, saved automatically, or the last saved version. There's little reason not to open the most recent version. If you open it and then decide you want the last saved version instead, close the note without saving it and open the saved version. If the note had never been saved, you'll simply be asked if you want to recover the note. Choosing No will permanently delete the note.

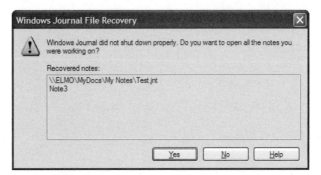

Figure 3-23   The File Recovery dialog box appears when Journal quits unexpectedly and there were unsaved changes.

By default, Journal saves your notes for automatic recovery every three minutes. You can increase or decrease this interval on the Other tab of the Journal Options dialog box.

> **Note**   If you know that Journal might recover a lost note when it opens, open Journal using the icon in the Start menu or Quick Launch bar, rather than opening the note file directly. If you open the last saved version of the same note Journal is trying to recover, you may lose all the unsaved changes.

Key Points

- Treat the Journal page as much like real paper as possible.
- Customize your pens and highlighters to match your work habits.
- Use the stroke eraser as your default eraser tool.

- Calibrate your screen size.

- Ink automatically groups as you write, but you can manually control grouping as needed.

- Use clever selection techniques to select just the ink you want.

- Write at 100% zoom if you plan to print your notes.

- Use note list to organize and clean out old notes.

Part II

Power Tablet Use

"When I sent out an e-mail announcement for a technical writer using a handwritten annotation at the top of the job announcement, the response I got was incredible. People who weren't even applying for the job wrote back to me to tell me how it was the coolest announcement they had ever seen."
—Suzanne Sowinska, Tablet PC Team

4

Formatting Windows Journal Notes and Adding Graphics

One of the great advantages of Windows Journal over a paper pad is the ability to reformat and manipulate ink after you have laid it down on the page. Formatting ink is similar to formatting text in an application such as Microsoft Word. Journal also allows you to add typed text and to insert pictures into notes. Similar to Word, Journal supports the concept of templates. You can use built-in templates or create custom templates to assist in creating notes.

Formatting Ink

Formatting ink is easily done using the Format toolbar. To display the Format toolbar, open the View menu and select Format from the Toolbars submenu. Select the ink you want formatted, and tap a button on the Format toolbar to apply bold, italic, or a different color. Bold increases the width of the ink stroke relative to the width of the original stroke, which means bold is subtle on very fine and extra fine pens, looks best on fine and medium pens, and is very extreme on thicker markers. Similarly, italic looks best on finer pens and gets difficult to read with markers. Changing the color will not change the shape or the width of the ink stroke. Figure 4-1 shows the Format toolbar and examples of ink formatted with bold and italic.

Format toolbar

Figure 4-1 Bold and italic formatting is applied to copies of identical pen strokes.

Formatting and Highlighting

If you select ink you have highlighted, both the ink and the highlighting are selected. This is necessary so that the highlighting will move and resize with any changes you make to the underlying ink. The highlight color is unaffected by changes to the color of the underlying ink, so if you change the ink color to red, the highlight color will not change. It is possible to change the color of the highlighting by tapping the highlighted area where it covers only blank paper. This selects only the highlighting which will now change when you select a new color from the Format toolbar.

Format Dialog Box

You may also format ink through the Format Ink command on the Edit menu. In addition to applying bold, italic, and color, the Format Ink dialog box, shown in Figure 4-2, lets you change the thickness of the ink stroke. The Format Ink dialog box also offers a one-step process to apply the thickness and color from one of the five pens in the Pen toolbar to the selected ink.

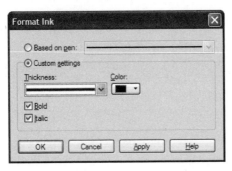

Figure 4-2   The Format Ink dialog box is an alternative way to format ink.

> **Tip**   Use a right-tap or a right-drag to simultaneously select the ink you want to format and open a shortcut menu containing the Format Ink command.

Formatting and Grouping

If the formatting does not apply as you expected, make sure the ink strokes are grouped as a word. Figure 4-3 shows the effect of italic formatting on ungrouped ink. The left-hand image is before formatting and the right-hand is after. Italic was applied to the whole word, but the top of the "I" was not formatted because Journal didn't consider it part of the group.

Figure 4-3   Formatting may not work correctly on ungrouped ink strokes.

Changing Pen Colors

Tapping a color on the Format toolbar with the pen tool and without any ink selected changes the color of that pen. You can think of it as "dipping" your pen in that color ink. This is very handy for changing pen colors quickly and works for highlighters as well as for pens. The only catch is that the new color is saved as the default for that pen. For example, if you have a blue medium point pen as the first one of your five custom pens and you dip the pen in green, your first custom pen is now a green medium point and will remain green until you change it again.

> **Tip**   If you like having several different pens on hand, using the Format toolbar for selecting pen color lets you use a greater combination of pen types and colors more easily. First customize your five pens for different widths and tips, but ignore the color. Then select the pen size and tip from the Pen menu, and select the color from the Format toolbar.

Custom Colors

In addition to the colors provided on the Format toolbar, you can use custom colors. Even if you don't use more than a few colors to write with, you may want a special color for drawings or text. Custom colors are also helpful when creating your own templates and stationery. To add a custom color to the Format toolbar, tap the **More Colors** button on the toolbar to display the Color dialog box shown in Figure 4-4. Select the color you want from the extended list on the left or the precision palette on the right, and tap Add To Custom Colors for each new color you want. The new colors appear in the Format toolbar once the dialog box closes.

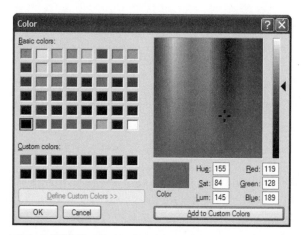

Figure 4-4   The Color dialog box allows you to add custom colors to the Format toolbar.

Change Shape

For most handwritten notes, straight lines and neat circles are not important, but for maps, diagrams, and notes you share, neatness may matter. If you need to clean up the shapes in your notes, you can convert the hand-drawn shapes to neater computer-drawn shapes using the Change Shape To command on the Actions menu. To change a shape, you must first select it. Since shapes are often in the midst of other text, this is usually best done by tapping the shape with the Selection Tool. It is very important that you select only the shape you want changed. Any additional selected ink will be deleted. You may have to ungroup the shape you want selected from other ink to select exactly what you want. Once the shape is selected, choose the desired final shape from the Change Shape To submenu. If the shape is a square, a circle, or an ellipse, it will be geometrically perfect. If the shape is a line, the new line may retain some of the curves in the original ink but will be primarily straight. After changing, the shape remains selected so that you can adjust its position and size to better fit your note. Figure 4-5 shows a before and after example for changing shapes.

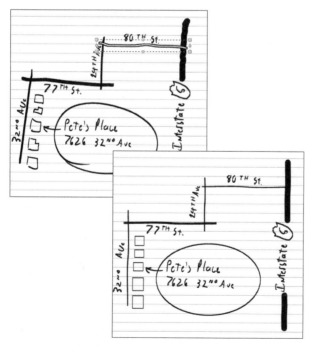

Figure 4-5   Select hand-drawn shapes and change them to computer-drawn shapes to clean up your images.

> **Caution**   When changing a shape that surrounds other ink, such as circled handwriting, be sure to select only the surrounding shape. When the shape is changed, all other selected ink is deleted.

Extended Shortcut Menu

Changing many shapes in a note can be a tedious task if you must continually select the type of shape you want from a submenu on the Actions menu. To streamline the process, you can add the Change Shape To commands (as well as several other useful commands) to the shortcut menu that appears when you right-tap. On the View tab in the Journal Options dialog box, check Show Extended Shortcut Menus to make the extra commands available. Figure 4-6 shows the default shortcut menu and the extended shortcut menu.

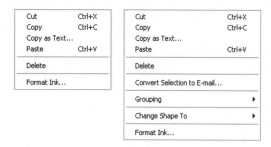

Figure 4-6   The extended shortcut menu on the right can make it easier to change shapes.

Adding Text and Pictures

Although it's very handy to just write and draw in Journal, sometimes you want to add typed text or pictures to your notes. Typed text in Journal notes are contained in rectangular areas called text boxes. You can also insert pictures of various file formats into your notes.

Using Text Boxes

There are three ways to create text boxes and put typed text in your note. The first one is to select handwriting in the note and convert it to text as was discussed in Chapter 3. After the conversion, one of your options is to replace the original ink with a text box. The second option is to copy text from another document and paste it into your note. The pasted text automatically appears in a text box. The third option is to insert a blank text box using the Insert menu. After inserting a blank text box, you can add text by using the Input Panel or a standard keyboard or by pasting.

Once the text box is in the document, it can be selected and moved just like any other object. To select the entire text box, tap the edge of the text box. The boundaries of the text box will appear, but there will be no flashing cursor inside. To make the flashing cursor appear amidst the text, tap the text. To select the text inside the text box, drag over the words you want selected. Figure 4-7 shows a text box with portion of that text selected.

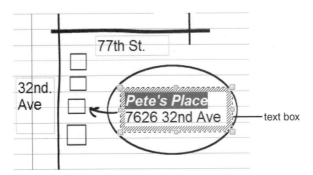

Figure 4-7   Some text is selected inside a text box.

When a text box is selected, a Format Text command replaces the Format Ink command on the Edit menu. Choosing Format Text opens the Font dialog box shown in Figure 4-8. Exactly which text is affected by the Font dialog box depends on what you selected. If you drag the cursor to select part of the text in a text box, as shown in Figure 4-7, only that text is changed. If you select the entire text box rather than the text within it, all the text in the text box is affected. If you select several text boxes with the Selection Tool, all the text boxes are affected.

> **Note**   You cannot simultaneously format text and ink.

Using text in a note is useful when creating diagrams or maps, especially if the writing must be small. There are a few limitations you should know. Ink always appears in front of text boxes, so be careful not to obscure your text with ink. If you resize a group of text and ink to better fit on the page, the text will not reduce in font size automatically. It's usually best to make all the text smaller first and then resize the drawing. Text in textboxes also can't be rotated, so labeling tall, thin items on a drawing may take some creativity.

Figure 4-8   If text or a text box is selected, a Font dialog box replaces the Format Ink dialog box.

Tip   You can change the color of text using either the Font dialog box or the Format toolbar; however, the dialog box offers only sixteen color options, while the Format toolbar offers millions using custom colors.

Note   The default text box font and size are set on the Note Format tab of the Journal Options dialog box.

Inserting Pictures

Notes may contain pictures from clip art, digital cameras, Web sites, or virtually any other digital picture source. To add a picture to your note, either choose the Picture command from the Insert menu, or simply drag the picture file onto the note. Once the picture is inserted, you can select, move, or resize it just like any other object in the note. Ink will always appear in front of the picture, just as it does when used with text boxes. This is handy if you want to draw on the picture, as shown by my son's party invitation in Figure 4-9. Pictures added to a note are stored as part of the note file. If you plan to share the note with anyone, avoid pictures that take up a lot of disk space, especially if you plan to send the note via e-mail.

Tip   If you want to insert a picture of an entire document, such as a fax, into a note and mark it up with comments, use the Import command on the File menu, described in Chapter 5, rather than Insert Picture.

Figure 4-9   Pictures always appear behind any ink.

Arranging and Deleting Text Boxes and Pictures

Text boxes and pictures are always behind the ink, but text boxes and pictures can be in front of or behind each other depending on the order in which they were inserted. The last object inserted is always on top. Journal does not have commands to send an object behind others or bring it to the front, so ideally you will insert the items you want in the background first. If you need to bring an object forward, the easiest thing to do is select the object, cut it, and then paste it again. The object will now be in front of all the others. If you want to permanently remove a text box or a picture, you must select it and cut or delete it. The eraser tool only affects ink.

> **Tip**   If you right-tap in Journal with nothing selected, the shortcut menu that appears contains options for inserting a text box, a picture, a flag or extra space or for selecting the entire page.

Setting the Page Properties

Changing the paper size, the rules, or the color of your note is done through the Page Setup dialog box. To open the Page Setup dialog box, choose Page Setup on the File menu. The Page Setup dialog box has options organized into four areas: paper, style, background, and title. These options allow you to create different paper pads for specific kinds of note-taking.

- **Paper**   The Paper tab sets the size and orientation of the page. Several standard page types are available, or you can create your own custom page. While the paper can be as large or as small as you want, if it is wider than the screen of your tablet you will need to either scroll left and right to see the whole page or write on the page while viewing it zoomed out, which results in extra-large handwriting if you print the note. I found that a custom size of 5.5 inches by 8.5 inches (one-half a letter-size page) fit well on my tablet screen and was convenient to print when I printed two per page. If you never print your notes and you want a continuous scrolling page instead of several sheets, you can make the paper up to four feet long!

- **Style**   The Style tab sets the position, the thickness, and the color for the page rules as well as for the paper color. Standard rule schemes such as college-ruled or large-graph are available, as well as custom settings. My custom 5.5–by–8.5-inch page is based on a narrow-ruled page with the margin line moved closer to the left side of the page. Setting all the lines to None results in a totally blank page.

> **Tip**   Use a rule setting that fits your normal handwriting size when the view is set for Page Width or 100% zoom, whichever setting you normally use.

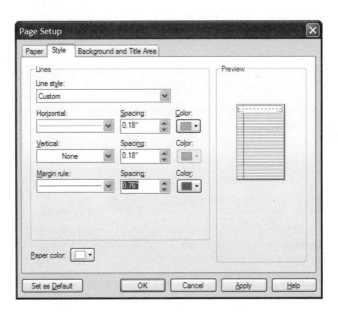

- **Background**   The Background section of the Background And Title Area tab lets you place a picture on the page, similar to the way you can place a picture on your Windows desktop. Pictures can be centered on the page, stretched to fill the page, or tiled so that the same picture repeats until the page is filled. You can also place the picture in the upper left or upper right for a letterhead effect. Top left and right background pictures will not stretch or move if the page is made longer using the Insert/Remove Space command, whereas centered or stretched pictures will.

  Many backgrounds come with Journal to simulate different paper textures and styles. Several of the more complicated Journal templates, such as blank music paper, are created by tiling a small picture in the background. Depending on the type of picture, you will want it more or less transparent. Less transparency is best if you need the picture to guide your writing, such as with music paper. More transparency is best with textures and backgrounds used for

effect. You can also supply your own background using most common file formats but, as with inserted pictures, use small files whenever possible.

Glossary   A *background* is a picture that appears behind ink,
text boxes, and inserted pictures. Backgrounds appear on
every page.

Tip   You can create your own watermark by placing your
name or company logo as a centered picture and making it
mostly transparent.

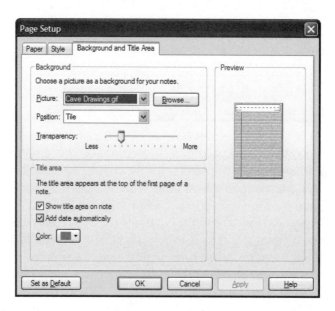

- **Title Area**   The Title Area section of the Background And Title Area
  tab lets you can turn on or off the note title area and the option to
  show the note's creation date. If you turn off the title area, however,
  the note filename appears in the note list pane instead of your handwritten title.

> **Tip**   If you want all new notes to open with your custom settings, tap the Set As Default button in the Page Setup dialog box. All new notes will open with your new settings.

Templates

Journal templates are essentially pads of Journal note paper or stationery. When you create a new note from a template, you open a copy of the template file, and the original remains untouched. The new note opens with a blank name and is saved as a new Journal note. Templates are a great system for keeping a wide array of paper types on hand.

> **Glossary**   A *template* is a file that contains the appearance and settings for a new Journal note. In a custom template, you can choose whether to include ink, pictures, and text boxes and whether to make these objects editable.

Using Built-In Templates

To create a new note using a template, choose the New Note From Template command from the File menu. By default, the Open dialog box will show the templates in your My Notes folder in your My Documents folder. Select the template you want, and tap Open. The templates shipped with Windows XP Tablet PC Edition include some custom paper types such as Genko sheets (for East Asian languages) and music paper, as shown in Figure 4-10. In addition to these options, more templates may become available from the Tablet PC Web site at *http://www.microsoft.com/tabletpc/*

> **Caution**   Opening a template file, instead of creating a new note from the template using the File menu, opens the original file. If you make changes and save them, they will be permanently added to the template.

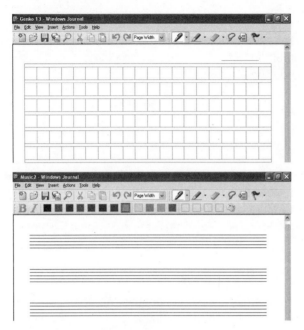

Figure 4-10 Templates offer a wide array of paper types.

Setting a Default Template

If you want a template to open as your default new note, open Journal Options from the Tools menu. On the Note Format tab, select the Note Template option and select the template you want, as shown in Figure 4-11. After you apply the changes, all your new notes will use the template. This is a great option if you create a custom template to serve as your personalized note paper.

Figure 4-11 Set a default template on this tab.

> **Note**   When Journal automatically recovers a note after a crash, the template background may be lost. If this happens, you can either add the background back in using Page Setup or copy the recovered ink onto a new note.

Creating Custom Templates

There are dozens of potential uses for custom templates, ranging from the simple to the very complex. The possibilities are endless, but here are some examples:

- A different background or page color
- A personalized note pad with your name or a small picture
- Letterhead
- A shopping list with check boxes for regularly purchased items
- A form you must complete on a regular basis
- A blank floor plan for a room you plan to remodel so that you can sketch out different options

Custom templates can contain pictures, text boxes, and ink. Any Journal note file can become a template simply by saving that note as a template. In fact, the only difference between a note file and a template is the extension on the filename. Journal notes are .jnt files and templates are .jtp files.

Creating a New Template

Creating a new template could be as easy as making a slight change to an existing file and saving it as a template, or it could be a several-step process. As an example of how you might make a more complicated template, here are the steps involved in creating a simple expense report.

1. Use the New Note From Template command to open the Blank template. The Blank template does not have any lines or images on the page.

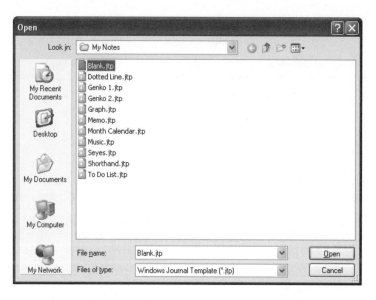

2. Open the Page Setup dialog box and set the paper size to Letter.

3. Sketch out form elements. The report needs a place to write the project accruing expenses and the types and dates for the expenses.

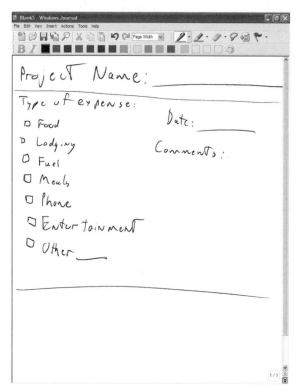

4.   Convert the handwriting to text. Since this template will be used over and over again, it is worth taking the time to make it more readable. Also the text will take up less space.

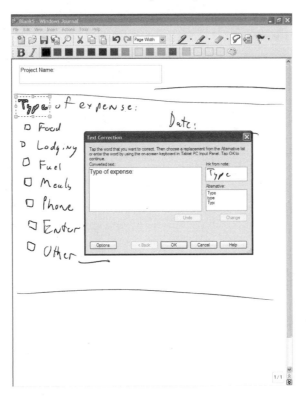

5.   Format and arrange the text. Use the Format Text command to get the look you want, and move the text boxes into the best position.

6.   Zoom in on detail objects to clean up and correct size. Once the object is the way you want, use copy and paste to repeat it. Leave a little space after the end of the words in a text box to prevent them from wrapping.

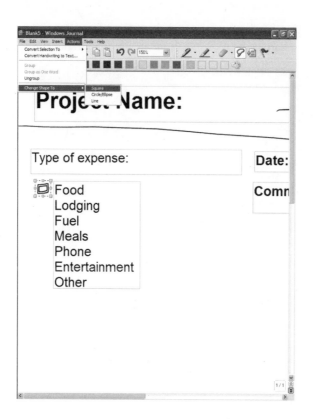

> **Tip**   To help align text boxes and objects, you can temporarily use the Grid background. You can set the background on the Background And Title Area tab of the Page Setup dialog box.

7.   Group objects to preserve positioning when copying and pasting. Once you see how they fit on the page, you may want to delete copies, edit the original for a better fit, and try copying again. Add any finishing touches, such as clip art or colors.

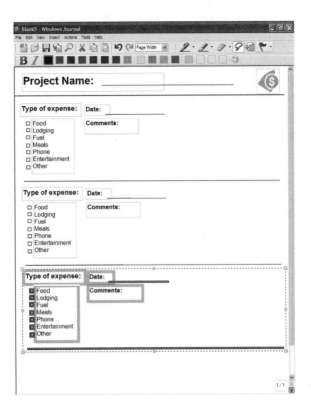

8.   When finished, save the note as a template.

When you save a note as a template, you must specify whether you want the ink, text, and pictures on the new note editable or not. If you make them available for editing, then the form you just created appears exactly as you saved it on new notes, but the user can select and change any of the objects. If you make them unavailable for editing, then the template becomes an unselectable, static image on the surface of the paper. You may also save only the stationery and background. Stationery refers to the settings made in the Page Setup dialog box and background refers to any background image. Ink, pictures, and text boxes are not saved when this option is selected. This option is handy if you have created a note page format while you were writing a note and want to keep the format of the page but not any of the notes on top. Figure 4-12 shows the dialog box that appears when saving a note as a template.

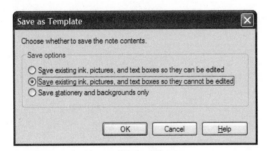

Figure 4-12   When saving a note as a template, you must specify save options.

> **Glossary**   *Stationery* refers to page settings for Journal notes, which include paper size, line and space settings, and background picture settings.

Creating TIFF and Metafile Backgrounds

A new note made from a template built by inserting ink and objects on the page, such as our expense report, shows only those objects on the first page. So if you created a new note from the expense report template, filled the first page, and started a second page, the new page would be blank. For objects to appear on every page, you must make those objects into a background picture, which means exporting them as a picture.

Export to TIFF

If you want to convert a Journal note directly into a picture, one option is to export it as a Tagged Image File Format (TIFF) file. This is not the most space-efficient file format for complex pictures and graphics, but it works well for simple pages with lots of white space. TIFF files work best at only one size and often look fuzzy or rough if resized too large or too small on the page. They are also only black and white, so any colors in your note are lost. Here are the steps to export the expense report and put it back into a template as a background:

1.   With the template open in Journal, select Export As from the File menu. The default export option is a Web archive file (.mht), discussed in Chapter 5. Select TIFF format, and tap Export.

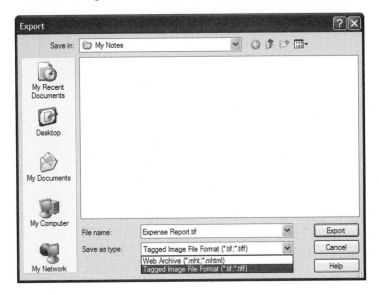

2.   Create a new note based on the Blank template. Set the paper size to letter. On the Background And Title Area tab of the Page Setup dialog box, set the background to the TIFF file you exported and set the position to either Center or Stretch. Because the TIFF file was the same size as the page you are placing it on, it should be a perfect fit.

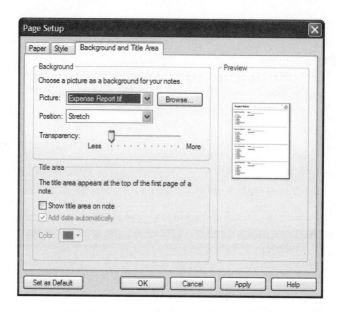

3.   Save the note as a template. Since the form is now in the background, any of the three save options will include the form. New notes created from this form will have the form on the first page and all subsequent pages.

Background and foreground objects can be used in conjunction as well. For example, you could make the form part of the expense report a background and put a "Project Name" text box as the header on the page. You could also include ink or pictures in this header. If this file was saved as a template, the header would appear only on the first page, but the form would appear on every page.

Creating Metafiles

Journal is great for sketching out a template, but several other programs do a better job of creating backgrounds. Microsoft PowerPoint and other applications can save pictures in Windows Metafile (.wmf) and Enhanced Windows Metafile (.emf) formats. These file formats are pictures, like the TIFF format, but they are much more space-efficient and produce good results even if resized. Much of the clip art supplied with Office is in a metafile format. If you have the option of either format, choose the Enhanced Windows Metafile option. Figure 4-13 shows a picture created in PowerPoint. To save a PowerPoint presentation as a metafile, select Save As from the File menu and select the metafile type. If the presentation has multiple slides, you will have to specify whether to save the current slide or every slide as a metafile. You can also save selected objects on a slide as a metafile by right-tapping the selected objects and choosing the Save As Picture command on the shortcut menu. Once saved as a metafile, the picture can be inserted as the background for new notes. Because it is a metafile, it will look sharp no matter how large or small the paper size of the note. You can use metafile pictures for whole-page images or small objects on the page as well.

Tip   Using the metafile format is a good way to make a form if you do not already have a form designed. If you want to convert an existing form into a Journal note, see Chapter 5.

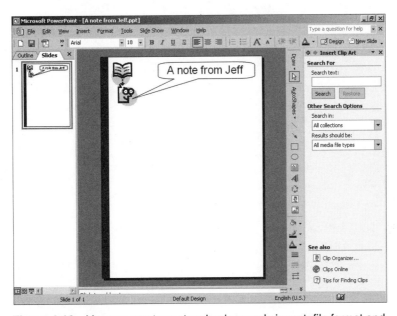

Figure 4-13   You can create custom backgrounds in metafile format and insert into Journal.

Tips for Custom Templates

Custom templates are a fun and powerful feature of Journal. Here are a few more tips for creating custom templates:

- Once you save a template with non-editable items, you can't edit the template. When you build a template, save it as a note rather than as a template while you are working on it. When you are done, save the note first, and then save it again as a template. Use the template on a regular basis, but keep the note as a source file in case you need to create a new version of the template in the future.

- To create a template with editable and non-editable items, first create a note containing only the non-editable items, and save it as a non-editable template. Next open a new document using that template, add the editable items, and save it as an editable template.

- If the template is more than one page long, such as a two-page form, new notes made from that template will open with multiple pages.

- If you create a template with the notes list pane open, a new note based on that template also opens the notes list pane.

- Remember that all the pictures you use are stored in the template. Avoid pictures that take up a lot of disk space as you will end up with many large note files.

- Only background pictures can tile or stretch automatically. Inserted pictures cannot.

- If you use background pictures rich in color, make them very transparent.

- If you like a piece of clip art, but it isn't quite right, you can often edit it in Paint or another application. If possible, save the picture as in a metafile format.

- The Microsoft Clip Organizer tool in Microsoft Office and the Microsoft Design Gallery Live Web site (http://dgl.microsoft.com) is a great source of artwork. Refer to the End User License Agreement (EULA) or documentation accompanying the product to see if your intended use falls within the terms of the agreement.

- If you unintentionally mess up a Journal template file, backup copies of all the templates that came with Journal are kept in Program Files\Windows Journal\Templates

> **Try This**   Here's a cool Journal trick. You can use a template to create game boards with movable pieces. During the development of Journal, someone made a full chessboard. The board was a centered background picture, and the pieces were drawn in two different colors of ink. He saved the template with the pieces in position for a new game. When he creates a new note from the template, the game is ready to play. He and his opponent move the pieces around, save the note to save the game, and delete it when they are done!

■ Try making a template for tic-tac-toe. (It's a bit simpler to draw than chess.) First make just the board, and play games by drawing in ink. Next try making Xs and Os that start on the side of the board and that players can move around. If that worked well, try making checkers!

Key Points

■ Tapping a color on the Format toolbar changes the pen or highlighter color if nothing is selected.

■ Select only the shape you want to convert and no extraneous ink.

■ Text boxes and pictures always appear behind ink.

■ Pictures are stored as part of the note, so try to keep them as small as possible. Use the metafile format for pictures where possible.

■ Use templates for a supply of custom paper types.

■ If you insert an object on a template it appears on the first page only. Background pictures appear on every page.

5

Annotating, Sharing, and Organizing Windows Journal Notes

Windows Journal has many useful features, but some are easy to overlook if you don't know they are there. For example, you can import documents created in various applications into Journal. Although you can't modify the imported documents, you can annotate them. If necessary, you can export notes as graphic files to share notes with people who don't have tablets. The search capabilities of Journal include ink, text boxes, and imported text. You might also discover that Journal can be useful for presentations and meetings.

Importing and Annotating Documents

Document import and annotation is one of Journal's coolest and most useful features. The Import command is really a Print command. When you import a document into Journal, you essentially print it onto Journal paper, which becomes the background for a new document. You can then use your pen, highlighter, and eraser tools to mark up the pages just as you would a real page. The page is more than just a digital printout, however. You can store multiple versions of the same document. You can even search the imported text, which is something you can't do on real paper. Once you have marked up the document, you could e-mail the final product to someone in full color, even if they don't have a Tablet PC and Journal. Microsoft Word documents, Web pages,

Microsoft PowerPoint slides, and pictures are all importable. If you can print it, you can import it into Journal.

To import a document into Journal, tap the **Import** button on the Standard toolbar or select Import from the File menu. Once you select the file to import, Journal will open the program used to read that file. The first time you import a file into Journal, a dialog box appears reminding you that Journal must open the original program to print the file into a Journal note and that the original program must be installed on your computer. This Import dialog box is shown in Figure 5-1. If the program that created the file is not installed on your computer, you may have trouble importing the note. For example, if you're sent a WordPerfect document and you use Word, you may need to open the document in Word and save it as a Word file before importing it into Journal. The dialog box appears every time you import a note until you check the Don't Show Me This Again check box.

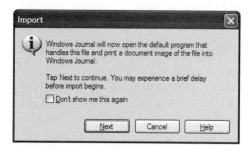

Figure 5-1 When importing a document into Journal, the document will be opened in its default program.

Imported documents always open as a new note with the same page dimensions as the original document. Because many of the files you will import will be 8.5-by-11-inch pages, the text may appear rather small on the tablet screen. Adjust the view setting as you work to show the whole page as you scan through the document, and zoom in when you need to see the text more clearly. Reading view is especially helpful when you're scanning a multi-page document. The contents of the imported document are treated identically to a non-editable picture on a Journal template. You can write ink and insert text boxes or pictures on the surface of the imported material, but you cannot select or change it. Figure 5-2 shows an example Journal note created from an imported Word document and annotated with pens and highlighters. Even though the imported document is non-editable, it is not a background image, so it will print even when the option for printing backgrounds is unchecked.

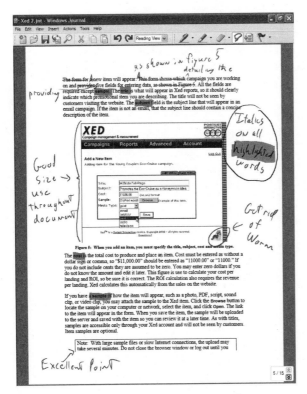

Figure 5-2   Mark up imported documents just as you would real paper.

Try This   The next time you need to fill out a form using a file on your computer, rather than printing it and filling it out, import it into Journal. Use Journal to fill out the form, taking advantage of the ability to correct mistakes and convert your handwriting to text if needed. When you are done, you can print out the form already completed and save a copy for your records. If it's a form you use regularly, you can make it into a template.

Importing by Printing to Journal Note Writer

Another way to import documents into Journal is to use the Journal Note Writer driver. If you're working in an application (such as Word) and you want to use the current document in Journal, you can print the document and select Journal

Note Writer as the printer as shown in Figure 5-3. Instead of printing the document, Journal will convert the document to a Journal note file. You'll be given the opportunity to specify name and location of the Journal note file. Once the Journal note file is created, it is automatically opened in Journal. Printing to Journal Note Writer has exactly the same result as the Import command but doesn't require opening Journal first.

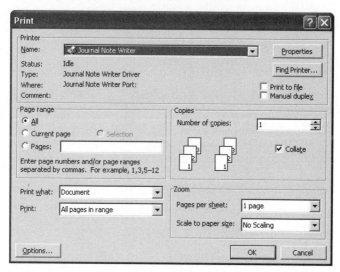

Figure 5-3   Printing to Journal Note Writer is another way to import documents into Journal.

Inserting Pages and Space on Imported Documents

Adding pages to imported documents works similarly to other Journal notes. To add more pages after the imported pages, tap the Next/New Page button, and to insert pages before the page you're viewing, select New Page from the Insert menu. The new pages will have the same style and background used for your new notes, but they will have the paper size of the imported page. So, if your notes are normally on 5.5-by-8.5-inch graph paper and the document you imported was 8.5 by 11 inches, then all pages you add to the imported document will be 8.5-by-11-inch graph paper. If you want to customize how additional pages appear, you can change the size and format of the paper using Page Setup. Journal will not change the size of the imported pages, however, so your Journal note will contain two different page sizes.

The Insert/Remove Space tool works a bit differently on pages with imported documents. Since the document itself is not editable, the Insert/Remove Space tool will move your ink but leave the underlying imported document untouched. This can wreak havoc on your annotations, as shown in Figure 5-4. There is no option to make the page longer when using the Insert/Remove Space tool on an imported document. If you push items off the bottom of the page, they will automatically move onto a new blank page.

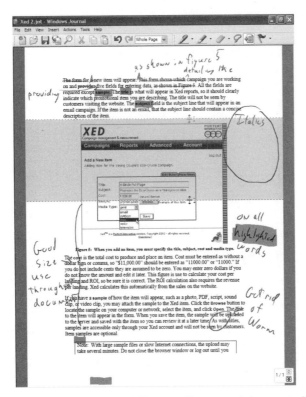

Figure 5-4   The Insert/Remove Space tool does not affect the underlying imported document.

Document Import Options

Sometimes documents will not import correctly using the standard Import command. This could be the result of missing fonts or linked files on your computer or peculiarities of the original program. If you experience problems importing a document, you can try importing the document as an image instead. Importing the document as an image will take longer, and you won't be able to search the imported document text. Searching notes will be discussed in "Searching Notes" later in the chapter.

To import documents as images, open the Journal Options dialog box and tap the File Import Preferences button on the Other tab to display the Journal

Note Writer Properties dialog box. Switch the output format to Print As An Image, as shown in Figure 5-5. Once you have imported the file, be sure to switch the preference back. Importing files as images should be used only when necessary.

Figure 5-5   If importing a document the standard way doesn't work, you can try importing the document as an image.

> **Tip**   Windows XP and Journal use Microsoft ClearType technology to improve the readability of text on the screen. If you are having trouble reading a document in an application that does not support ClearType, try importing the document into Journal.
>
> To make sure ClearType is turned on, open the Display control panel, tap the Appearance tab, and tap the Effects button. In the Effects dialog box, make sure Use The Following Method To Smooth Edges Of Screen Fonts is checked and make sure ClearType is selected in the drop-down list.

Sharing Journal Files

If you want to share a Journal note with another tablet user, just send them the note. All the information, including ink, imported documents, text boxes, and pictures are saved in the note file. If you want to share your Journal notes with someone who does not have a tablet, and therefore does not have Journal, you must export the note either as a Web archive file (.mht) or as a Tagged Image File Format image (.tif).

Exporting a Note as a Web Archive File

Web archive files are essentially self-contained Web pages that include text and graphics in a single file. Web archive files are readable by Internet Explorer 5 or later, on both Windows or Macintosh platforms, and by most Microsoft Office programs. Web archive files are in color and can be a single page or multiple pages. When displaying Web archive files, Internet Explorer shows a bar above the page that includes navigation buttons, the current page number, and possibly a zoom drop-down list, as shown in Figure 5-6. To export a note as a Web archive file, select Export As on the File menu and select Web Archive as the file type.

Bar that appears when displaying Web archive files (.mht)

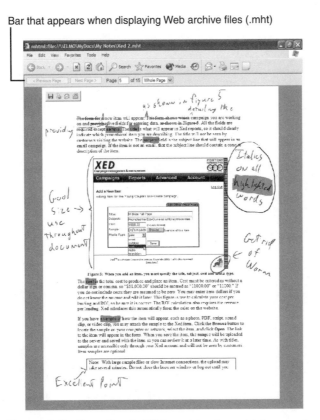

Figure 5-6   Exporting to Web archive format lets you share your files with people who do not have a tablet and Journal.

> **Tip**   If you have an office intranet, you can share Journal notes on the company Web site in Web archive format.

Exporting a Note as TIFF

As discussed in Chapter 4, notes can be exported as Tagged Image File Format (TIFF) files. These files are only in black and white, but they are readable by just about anyone. TIFF files also have a higher resolution than Web archive files and print better for notes containing predominantly text. Highlighted text and photographic images look terrible in the TIFF format—often so bad they are unreadable. TIFF files containing more than one page are also unreadable by some programs. In general, Web archive is the best format for sharing your Journal files, but if the Web archive file isn't working, you can try the TIFF format. To export a note in the TIFF format, select Export As on the File menu and select Tagged Image File Format as the file type.

Sending as E-Mail

If you are going to send a note by e-mail, you can make the process of exporting shorter by selecting Send To Mail Recipient on the File menu. Journal will ask which of three formats, Journal note, Web archive, or TIFF, you want to use, as shown in Figure 5-7, and then will create a blank e-mail message with the note already attached.

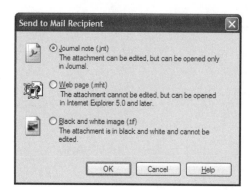

Figure 5-7   You have a couple of different options when using the Send To Mail Recipient command.

Searching Notes

As mentioned in Chapter 3, Journal performs background handwriting recognition on your ink as you lay it down on the page and stores the list of probable words and alternatives. The word list is used both for converting your ink to text and for finding words in your notes. When you search your notes using the Find command, Journal will show all items in which your search text matches the words it recognized or any of the top six alternatives. This "fuzzy find" is a bit of a trade-off. By finding alternatives, you are more likely to find the text you want, but you will also find several near misses. To search your current note for specific text, select Find from the Edit menu or tap the **Find** button on the Standard toolbar to make the Find pane appear, as shown in Figure 5-8.

Figure 5-8   Use the Find pane to quickly search for text in your note.

Tap the Look For field, and use Input Panel to enter your search text. Next tap Find. The first match in the document will appear selected. Continue searching the document by tapping Next until you find the text you want. Find is not case-sensitive and you cannot search for more than one word or phrase at a time. Figure 5-9 shows a typical search result in which the word "specific" is found correctly, but tapping Next finds the similar word "pacific."

> **Tip**   Find starts looking on whatever page you are viewing. If you want to search an entire note, either start your search from the first page or say yes when asked whether you want to continue your search from the beginning of the note.

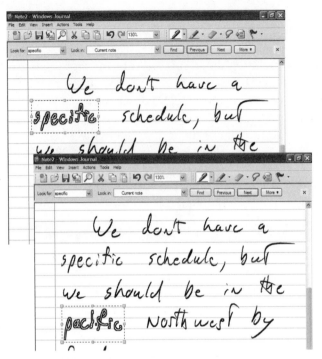

Figure 5-9   The Find command returns words that match or are similar to your search text.

Searching Within Text Boxes and Imported Documents

Text boxes and the imported document text can be included in the search as well, but the results will depend on how the text was inserted. Text boxes created from handwriting converted to text retain their alternate words list, so the fuzzy find still applies, and similar words are included in the results. If the text box contains text pasted from another program, there is no alternate list, and only exact matches are found. In either case, Find selects the entire text box, rather than a single word within it, but this usually isn't a problem because text boxes rarely contain more than a paragraph of text. If the note contains text imported via the Import command using the standard import, all the imported text is included, but only for exact matches. When one of these words is found, it appears highlighted. Documents imported as images, as well as any words contained within an image, are not included in the search. Figure 5-10 shows how ink, text boxes, and imported text would appear in a search for the word "campaign." In reality, only one of these found words would be selected at a time and you would use the Next and Previous buttons to move between them. Notice that the word "campaign" in the picture was not found by the search.

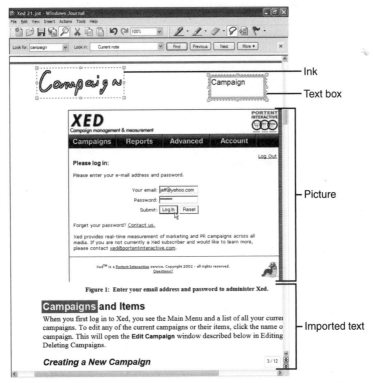

Figure 5-10   Here are examples of how search results appear for ink, text boxes, and imported text. Text in pictures cannot be searched.

Setting Search Options

If you don't want alternate words or the imported text included in your search, tap the More button on the right of the Find pane and uncheck the options for Include Close Matches or Include Document Image Text as needed. The expanded Find pane also provides an option for finding flags instead of text. The expanded Find pane is shown in Figure 5-11.

Figure 5-11   Use the expanded Find pane to specify additional search parameters.

Searching Across Multiple Notes

By default, Find searches only your current note. To search through multiple notes, enter the search text in the Look For field of the Find pane and then specify in the Look In field the folder or drive you want searched. If the Find pane is expanded, you'll notice that additional options are enabled. You have options to limit your search by specific dates and whether to search subfolders. After you specify your options and tap Find, the note list pane opens, showing all the notes that contain matches. Tapping any note in the note list opens that note at the place of the first match. Tapping Next finds the next match in that note. Once the end of the note is reached, tapping Next finds the first match in the next note on the list. Figure 5-12 shows an example search across multiple notes.

> **Note**   If you use the Search tool on the Start menu to search for text within documents, it will find matches to handwritten words, text boxes, and imported document text in Journal notes. It will see only the handwriting recognizer's most likely word, however, and not any of the alternates.

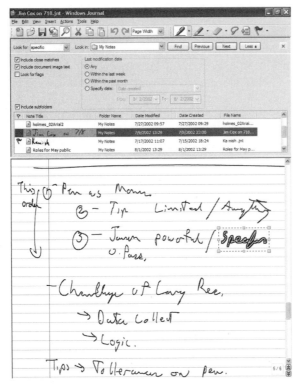

Figure 5-12   Your search results are listed in your current note.

Presentations and Meetings Using Journal

When it comes to making digital presentations, PowerPoint may have the corner on the market, but Journal can be a powerful presentation tool. In Chapter 6, we will explore the tools that the Office Pack for Tablet PC adds to PowerPoint, but even with the Office Pack installed, Journal offers much more sophisticated and flexible pen and highlighter tools, lets you switch quickly to a blank writing surface, and provides the ability to select and edit objects you just drew. If your presentation is highly interactive, Journal may be the best tool for the job. In fact, some of the business people testing tablets during development imported entire PowerPoint presentations into Journal just to take advantage of the pen and editing tools. Importing a document into Journal and then projecting it on a screen is also a great way to work collaboratively in a meeting.

Here are a few tips for getting the most out of Journal as a presentation and collaboration tool.

- **Switch to landscape orientation if you're using an LCD projector**   If you forget to do this it will be obvious when you turn on the projector and the image is sideways! Switching beforehand is less embarrassing.

- **Use full-screen view**   Full-screen view makes your presentation as large and visible as possible. Making the most of screen space is especially important when viewing portrait orientation documents on a landscape orientation screen, which most digital projectors require. Full-screen view also hides other distracting programs, the taskbar, and extra toolbars.

- **Customize the Journal toolbars**   When in full-screen view, Journal shows different default toolbars. If you're viewing landscape orientation documents, such as imported PowerPoint slides, arrange the toolbars onto one line to use less space. If you're viewing portrait orientation documents, consider turning off the toolbars altogether. All the commands to change pens and tools are still available through the menus.

- **Use reading view if appropriate**   Reading view is a great way to move through a document one page or one screen at a time. Either the down arrow or the Spacebar will advance you to the next page.

- **Display the page bar if appropriate**   The page bar shows all the pages in your note as numbered blocks, and you can jump to any page by tapping that block. This is very handy with large documents but can be distracting to your audience as they wonder what is on the upcoming slides.

Figure 5-13 shows an imported PowerPoint presentation in full-screen view with reading view and the page bar turned on.

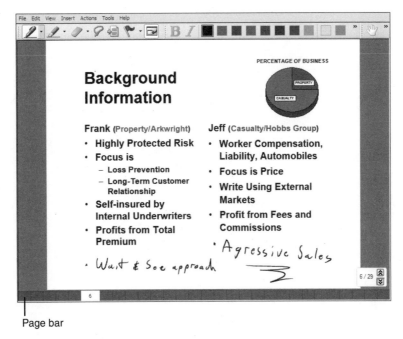

Page bar

Figure 5-13   Use full-screen view and the page bar when using Journal for presentations.

Key Points

- Import documents into Journal to annotate or fill out with a pen.

- You cannot insert space within imported documents.

- Export your notes to a Web archive for sharing with people who do not have Journal.

- The Find feature in Journal includes alternate words and imported text.

- Journal is a great presentation and meeting collaboration tool.

6

Microsoft Office and the Office XP Pack for Tablet PC

The Microsoft Office XP Pack for Tablet PC, or Tablet Pack, adds support for using ink directly in certain Microsoft Office XP applications (Microsoft Word 2002, Microsoft Excel 2002, Microsoft PowerPoint 2002, and Microsoft Outlook 2002). The Tablet Pack adds three new features to Office. The first, and most significant, is the *ink drawing and writing area*, which allows writing and drawing within certain Office documents. The second is a change to the slide show shortcut menu in PowerPoint, which provides pen tools during slide shows. The third is a set of information conduits to exchange information between Windows Journal and Outlook. In a sense, the Tablet Pack is a glimpse into the future, demonstrating how applications written with tablet users in mind will incorporate ink-enabled features. The Tablet Pack itself is an interim solution, and other Office applications such as Microsoft Access, Microsoft Visio, and Microsoft FrontPage are not enhanced by the Tablet Pack. Future versions of Office and other major applications will provide tablet-enabled features as part of the applications themselves. Someday you may be able to use your pen to annotate a document directly in Word as easily as you can when you import it into Journal. A piece of this future is available today with the Tablet Pack.

*When I sent out an e-mail announcement for a technical writer
using a handwritten annotation at the top of the job
announcement, the response I got was incredible. People who
weren't even applying for the job wrote back to me to tell me
how it was the coolest announcement they had ever seen.*
—Suzanne Sowinska, Tablet PC Team

> **Note**   Installing the Tablet Pack is strictly optional. Using your pen
> instead of a mouse and using Input Panel, you have full control over all
> Office applications. You can still insert ink into any Office document by
> drawing it in Journal, copying it, and pasting it into the document.

Download and Installation

The Tablet Pack is available as a free download from Microsoft. The U.S. English
version is available at http://go.microsoft.com/fwlink/?linkid=9132&clcid=0x409

Once the Tablet Pack installer is downloaded, close all Office applications
and Journal and double-tap the installer program. The installer will open and
guide you through the installation process. The only installation options are the
location of the Help files and the link to the video demonstrating the features of
the Tablet Pack, as shown in Figure 6-1.

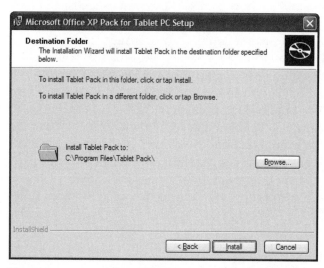

Figure 6-1   Specify the destination folder when installing the Tablet
Pack.

Tablet Pack Help is accessible from the Help menu of Office applications enhanced by the Tablet Pack. The Tablet Pack demo will open by default after the Tablet Pack is installed. If you don't want to view the demo, you can uncheck the Start The Tablet Pack Tutorial check box on the last installer screen.

> **Note**   Tablet Pack Help is not integrated into the main Help system for Office, so it will not be included in searches you conduct using the regular Help or the Office Assistant.

> **Note**   In addition to the Tablet Pack, you may need to add speech recognition to your Office applications for full tablet integration. Sometimes this feature is installed when Office is installed, and sometimes it is not. If when opening an Office document you are prompted to install speech recognition, insert your Office CD, and let the installer add these files. If you don't have access to your Office CD at that moment, you can postpone it, but every time you open a file that uses speech recognition, you will be asked about installation again.

The Ink Drawing and Writing Area

While the details of using ink vary between Office applications enhanced by the Tablet Pack, the tool that unites them is the *ink drawing and writing area* or just *ink area*. Writing and drawing in an ink area are fairly intuitive and do not require much explanation to use at a basic level. However, if you want full utility out of ink areas and want to avoid some potential frustrations, a little background understanding really helps. The ink area is an object. Objects are items other than text that you insert into your Office documents. Photos, clip art, sound files, even graphs from Excel are all objects. (If you want to see how many different kinds of objects are available in an Office application, select the Object command on the Insert menu and count them. My version of Word lists 29 different objects I could insert.) This distinction is important because text and objects are always separate. You can use only the pen to write or draw inside the border of an ink area. You cannot write, highlight, or draw on top of text and you cannot type text inside the border of an ink area. The concept of an object is also key for changing the format of an ink area. As we will see later in this chapter, the Format Object command is central for making the most of ink in Office.

The objects most people are familiar with are pictures. An ink area is actually similar to a picture in that you may resize it, drag it to a new position in the document, change the way text flows around it, group it with other objects, and in some cases add a border and fill color. Unlike a picture, you can write, draw, select, edit, and erase inside ink areas using pen tools similar to what you find in Journal. Figure 6-2 shows what an ink area looks like in Word.

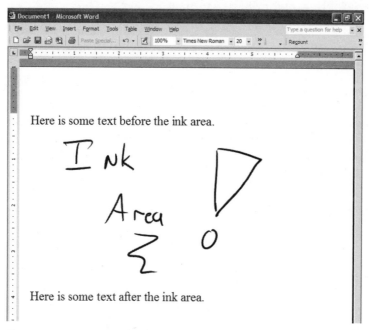

Figure 6-2 You can easily edit an ink area in Word.

Glossary An *ink area* is a rectangular object in an Office application enhanced by the Tablet Pack, where you can write, draw, select, edit, and erase using pen tools.

To insert an ink area into an Office application enhanced by the Tablet Pack, tap once to place the cursor where you want the ink area to appear and either tap the **Insert Ink Drawing And Writing** button on the Standard toolbar or select Ink Drawing And Writing from the Insert menu. A blank ink area appears with a floating Ink toolbar of pen tools as shown in Figure 6-3. Once you have drawn what you want inside the ink area, tapping anywhere outside the ink area border will deselect it. The blue hash-mark border will disappear, but the ink will remain as part of your document. To open and edit any ink area, tap the ink area once, and the blue border will reappear.

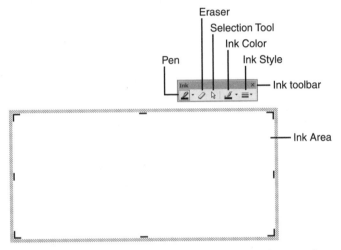

Figure 6-3   A blank ink area and the Ink toolbar of pen tools.

> **Note**   There is no option to undo inserting an ink area. To remove an ink area, you must select and cut or delete it.

Pens and Highlighters

The ink area provides six basic pens, three ball point and three felt tip, each available in three different colors, and three highlighters. All the pens have round tips, but the felt tip pens are slightly wider and are pressure sensitive if your tablet supports that feature. To switch pens, tap the triangle next to the

Pen button on the Ink toolbar, select a new pen from the list, and then start writing anywhere inside the boundaries of the ink area. As with Journal, highlighters let the underlying ink show through, but the color of the ink may shift, and the different highlight colors will mix where they touch.

You can create a custom pen width and color while using any of the six pens, but unlike the five user-defined pens in Journal, the changes are only temporary. If you're writing with a black felt-tip pen on an ink area and you change the color to green and the tip to six points wide, your pen will become a green marker. The pen will remain a green marker until you either customize the pen again or go back to using any of the six predefined pens or three highlighters. Once you reselect a predefined pen, your custom pen settings are discarded. Creating a custom pen in one Office application affects all the ink areas in that application but doesn't affect other Office applications. For example, if you create a green ballpoint pen in Word, every ink area in every document you have open will have a green ballpoint pen available, but ink areas in Outlook will not.

Custom pens inherit the properties of whatever pen was selected, so to create a custom highlighter you must start with a predefined highlighter. It doesn't matter which color you choose, however, because this is easily changed. Once you have selected the type of pen you want, choose a new color by tapping the triangle next to the Ink Color button on the Ink toolbar and make your selection from the list. To choose a new pen width, tap the Ink Style button on the Ink toolbar and make your selection from the list. Select any of the predefined pens when you are finished with the custom pen.

> **Note**   The Ink Color button is used to change the pen color. Although the Ink Color button has a paintbrush icon on it, you can't use this tool for drawing on the ink area.

> **Note**   The width of the predefined highlighter is wider than the maximum custom pen width of six points. If you make a custom highlighter, do not change the pen width unless you want a very narrow highlighter. Once you customize the highlighter width, six points is as wide as you can go until you reselect a predefined highlighter.

Erasing and Selecting

All erasing is done with the eraser tool. The eraser is always a stroke eraser. The stroke eraser allows for fast erasing, especially if you write in script in which the entire word is a single stroke, but you cannot touch up your strokes with the eraser as you can in Journal. There is no scratch-out gesture in an ink area, but there is a top-of-pen erase if your pen has that feature and the feature is enabled.

> **Caution**   There is no undo when editing ink on a ink area. If you delete or significantly change your ink, it is permanent.

The ink area Selection Tool is a marquee-type tool, rather than the lasso-type tool used in Journal. The difference is that a marquee selection is rectangular and is created by starting in one corner of the area you want selected and dragging the marquee until it contains the desired ink. Figure 6-4 shows the difference with selecting using the two selection tools. The marquee selection limits your precision when it comes to selecting specific ink strokes, but two special selection techniques can help. When you write words on an ink area, the ink strokes are grouped into words, just as they are in Journal. The marquee will select the word only if it encloses more than 50 percent of the ink strokes that make up the word. This allows you some leeway in getting only the text you desire. The second technique is to tap with Selection Tool to select a single ink stroke instead of dragging a marquee around it. Once you have ink selected, you can move, resize, cut and paste it, or change its color and width.

> **Note**   Even though ink strokes are grouped into words, there is no handwriting recognition of ink in ink areas The words in an ink area are not included when you search an Office document for specific text using the Find command.

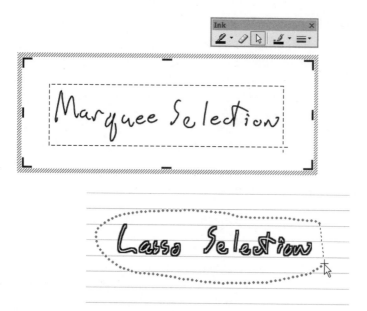

Figure 6-4   The Selection tool in action.

Selecting Ink and Ink Areas

One of the keys for power use of ink areas is understanding that there are three kinds of selections for your writing and drawings: ink selection, ink area selection, and object selection. With ink selection, you use the Selection Tool to select some or all of the ink inside the ink area. Once selected, this ink can be moved, resized, copied, or cut. With ink area selection, you tap the border of an ink area or tap inside on a spot free of ink. This selects the ink area *without selecting the ink it contains.* This lets you make the ink area larger when you need more room to draw or smaller so that it takes up less space in your document without changing the ink. (If you resize it smaller than the area occupied by ink, some of the ink will appear cropped.) With object selection, you tap or right-tap the blue border of an ink area you have already selected, and the border will change to a solid black line. You have now selected the ink area as an object. Resizing the ink area now will change the ink area *and* all the ink it contains. Selecting an ink area as an object is also required to adjust the border and layout for an ink area. Table 6-1 shows what each selection looks like and the effect of resizing.

Try This   This concept of three kinds of selection is much clearer once you do it yourself. Open a new Word document, and insert an ink area. Write a few words inside, and then try selecting and resizing the ink and ink area to get each of the effects shown in Table 6-1.

Table 6-1   The different kinds of selections and effect of resizing.

Ink selected   Ink resized

Ink area selected   Ink area resized

Object selected   Object resized

Copy and Paste with Ink Areas

The results of copying and pasting using ink areas are also very dependent on exactly what you have selected, both when you copy and when you paste. If you select an entire ink area in one Office document, copy it, and then paste it in a different location or into a different Office document, it will insert as an ink area that you can continue to edit. It doesn't matter whether you selected it as an ink area or as an object, so long as you selected the whole thing. If you select the ink in an ink area, instead of the ink area itself, it gets trickier. Taking selected ink from one ink area and putting it in another ink area is a three-step process.

1.   Select and copy the desired ink.

2.   Insert a new ink area into the document or select an existing ink area where you want the ink pasted.

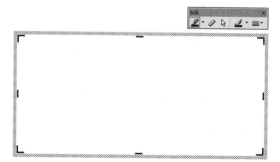

3.   Paste the ink into the ink area.

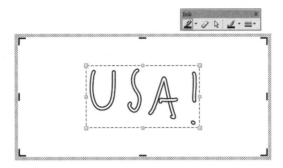

If you leave out step two and simply paste the ink into an Office document, without inserting a new or selecting an existing ink area, the ink will be converted into a picture. Once the ink becomes a picture, you can no longer edit it with pen tools. Pictures, however, offer far more formatting options than ink areas. Pictures can be made transparent and rotated, as shown in Figure 6-5. They are also easier to combine with other Office-drawn objects such as auto shapes and flow charts. This is where understanding the ins and out of ink areas pays off. As you work with ink in various Office applications, you can choose the format, ink or picture, that best meets your needs in each situation.

> **Tip**   If you paste ink as a picture, keep the original ink in a document somewhere until you are certain you have no more edits. It's really annoying to re-create ink to correct one tiny mistake.

Figure 6-5   The "USA" ink in an ink area (left) can be edited, but the formatting options are limited. The "USA" ink pasted in as a picture (right) cannot be edited, but offers greater format flexibility.

Copying and pasting between an ink area and Journal requires attention as well. If you are copying ink from Journal to an Office application, the same rules apply as when copying from an ink area. If you copy ink from Journal and paste it onto an ink area, it remains ink. If you copy ink from Journal and paste it directly into an Office application, it becomes a picture. Going the other direction (from Office applications to Journal), the rules are almost reversed. If you select the ink in an ink area, copy it, and paste it directly into Journal, it inserts as ink. If you select an entire ink area, however, and paste the ink area into Journal, it becomes a picture.

> **Tip** If you have a fairly complex drawing you want placed in an ink area, create the drawing in Journal where you have better tools. Once the drawing is complete, select, copy, and paste it into an ink area or directly into the Office document as a picture.

Paste Link

One very cool feature of ink areas is that they support Object Linking and Embedding (OLE). This means you can keep a master version of the ink area and then use the Paste Link command to copy that into other ink areas in other Office applications. For example, you might have a diagram you are developing in a Word document that you would like to use in a PowerPoint presentation. If you use the Paste Link command to bring the Word ink area into PowerPoint, then any changes you make in Word are automatically changed in PowerPoint.

> **Glossary** *Object Linking and Embedding*, or *OLE*, is a system for copying an object from one file—including text, ink drawing and writing, pictures, tables, and others—and pasting it into another file so that changes in the source appear automatically in the target. To use OLE, you must choose Paste Link from the Edit menu rather than the conventional Paste command.

To paste link an ink area, first select it as an object rather than as an ink area and choose the Copy command. Next place your cursor in the document where you want to paste the picture, but do not insert an ink area. Select Paste Special from the Edit menu, and choose Paste Link As An Ink Drawing And Writing Object, as shown in Figure 6-6.

The copied picture will appear exactly as it does in the first document. You can move and resize the linked copy, but you can edit the picture only in the original document. Once you save the new document, the complete picture is included, so you do not need the original to view the copy. However, each time you open the document containing the linked copy, you will see a dialog box, like the one shown in Figure 6-7, asking whether you want to update the link to the original. If the original is not available, the link cannot be updated.

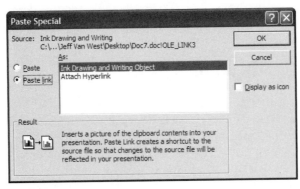

Figure 6-6   Using Paste Link allows you to keep one master version of an ink area.

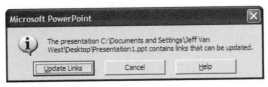

Figure 6-7   When opening a document that contains linked objects, you will be asked whether you want to update links.

> **Note**   Linked objects may not offer all format options such as transparency or rotation.

Compatibility with Other Versions of Office

The Tablet Pack works only with Office XP, so if you are using an older version of Office on your tablet, you must upgrade to take advantage of the Tablet Pack. The Tablet Pack also works correctly only under Windows XP Tablet PC Edition, so you cannot install it on a non-tablet computer running Office XP and use the features with a mouse instead of a pen.

The good news is that any documents you create that include ink areas are readable by Office XP without the Tablet Pack installed and older versions of Office for both Windows and the Macintosh. These users will see ink areas as pictures with all the color and formatting intact. They cannot edit the ink areas, but they can select, move, and print them. One caveat to this statement involves Outlook e-mail. When a message is forwarded, the ink area is converted to a placeholder that says "<<object>>". See the section "Using the Tablet Pack with Outlook" later in this chapter for more information.

Using the Tablet Pack with Word

The fundamentals of inserting and using an ink area are the same in Office applications enhanced by the Tablet Pack. The primary differences are how the ink area appears in the document and the options for formatting. When you insert an ink area in Word, it will expand out to the margins of the page and slightly more than half that distance high, with a solid white background and no border. It will also be in line with the text, so if you insert or remove text, the ink area will move to stay at the same place in your narrative. In most cases, these settings work fine. If you need a more complex layout, you can adjust the appearance of the ink area using the Format Object command.

Here's an example of how you might reformat an ink area in Word to integrate more smoothly with the text layout:

1. Insert a new ink area where you want it in the document.

2. Draw in the ink area and resize it as necessary.

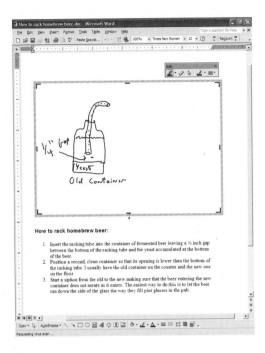

3. Format the ink area by selecting it and choosing Object from the Format menu or choosing Format Object from the shortcut menu. In this
case, the layout is changed to put the ink area behind the text so that
text can be formatted around the ink drawing.

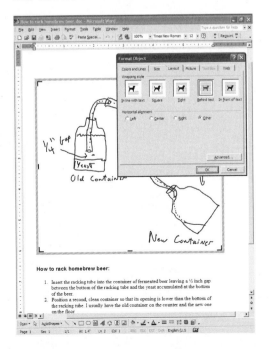

4. Reformat the paragraphs to flow around the text. (Alternatively, you can define boundaries on the drawing for text to flow around.)

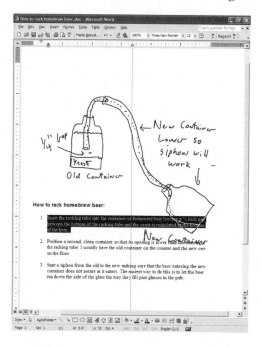

5. Save the final product.

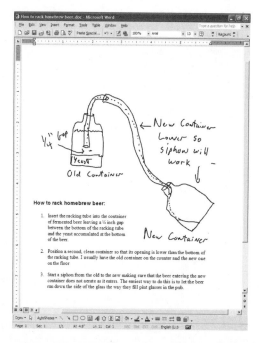

Changing the layout of the ink area so that it is no longer in line opens up several options, including putting colored borders around the ink area; grouping the ink area with other ink areas, pictures, or objects; and arranging which objects appear on top of others. In Figure 6-8, the picture and the ink area are set to a square layout so that they can be placed next to each other on the page and are being grouped into a single object using the Group command on the Drawing toolbar. As a group, these objects will stay together as the document is edited. The ink area also has a border around it to separate it from the text and make it easier to read.

> **Tip**   If the Drawing toolbar isn't visible, open it manually by selecting Drawing from the Toolbar submenu on the View menu.

Figure 6-8 Grouping ink areas and other objects maintains their positions relative to each other as you move them around your layout.

No matter how you format an ink area, you cannot make the fill color transparent. This can make mixing pictures, text, and ink areas difficult when the ink area is behind text and pictures because whenever you select the ink area to draw, the surrounding text and pictures disappear. Drawing ink on top of pictures is best done in Journal and pasted into Word as a picture. As shown back in Figure 6-5, pictures have more formatting flexibility than ink areas anyway.

Try This   Next time you need to create an invitation to a party or a function, try creating it in Word with clip art and a map drawn with the pen, as well as using typed text. Try creating the same invitation in Journal and compare the two. You'll probably find that manipulating ink and pictures was easier with Journal but adding and editing typed text was easier with Word. Once you have a better feel for each application, you can pick the one that best meets your needs for a particular job.

Ink in Word Comments

The Tablet Pack also lets you use ink in Word comments. This is a phenomenal feature if you are reviewing a Word document and don't have a keyboard available. Inserting an ink comment is done the same way as inserting a typed comment or voice comment. Select the point in the text where you want the comment to appear or select the block of text you are commenting on, and choose Ink Comment from the Insert menu or choose New Ink Comment from the Reviewing toolbar as shown in Figure 6-9.

Figure 6-9   Selecting New Ink Comment from the Reviewing toolbar.

An ink comment is actually just a shortcut for opening a normal comment and then inserting an ink area, so the same pen tools will appear. Write your comment, expanding or reducing the ink area as needed, and when you are done, tap anywhere outside the borders of the ink area. Since the ink comment is simply a comment window containing an ink area, you can mix ink and text in a comment by typing your text and then drawing in the ink area. Figure 6-10 shows how an ink comment, a typed comment, and a mixed comment appear in the document margin in Word.

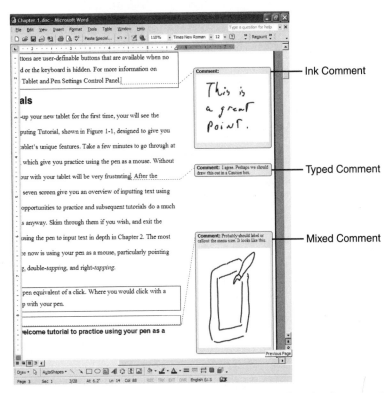

Figure 6-10   An ink comment, a typed comment, and a mixed comment in Word.

The bubble comments in the margin are a new feature in Word 2002. In previous versions of Word, comments were marked by a small footnote in the text but appeared in a separate window called the Comments pane. People viewing your ink comments with older versions of Office will see them in the Comments pane as pictures, as shown in Figure 6-11.

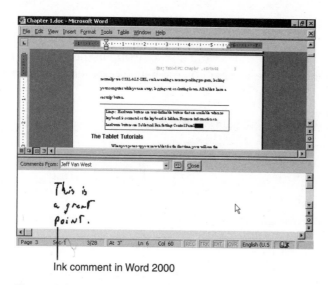

Ink comment in Word 2000

Figure 6-11   Ink comments appear in the Comments pane of older versions of Word.

Using the Tablet Pack with Excel

Ink areas in Excel are actually simpler than in Word and appear to the right of whichever cell you have selected. They are always free-floating elements, so after you create one, you can drag it to any location on your spreadsheet. As you add or remove cells, the ink area will move to remain in approximately the same position relative to adjacent cells. Excel ink areas are also transparent by default, so they will not obscure cells in your spreadsheet. The disadvantage of the transparency is that the ink strokes do not look as smooth. Figure 6-12 shows an ink area on an Excel spreadsheet. The "Total Due" cells are actually under the ink area. The transparent ink area is still in front of the cells in your spreadsheet, so if you try to tap a cell to edit its contents you will select the ink area instead. To get to cells under the ink area, you must use the arrow keys on Input Panel or on a standard keyboard or temporarily drag the ink area out of the way.

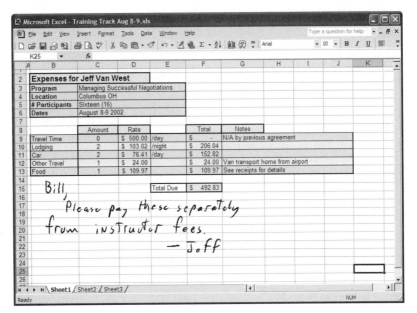

Figure 6-12   Ink areas in Excel are free-floating and have transparent backgrounds.

> **Note**   While an ink area is selected and you are writing on it, it will have an opaque, white background. Once you tap outside the border, it will become transparent again.

Formatting Options in Excel

If you want a border or background on your ink area in Excel, select the ink area as an object by either tapping the border twice or right-tapping the border and choose Format Object just as you did in Word. In the Format Object dialog box shown in Figure 6-13, use the Colors And Lines tab to select a fill color for a background and a line color for a border. If you create a border, you must also select a line style or weight. The default line weight is zero points, so if you only choose a color nothing will appear.

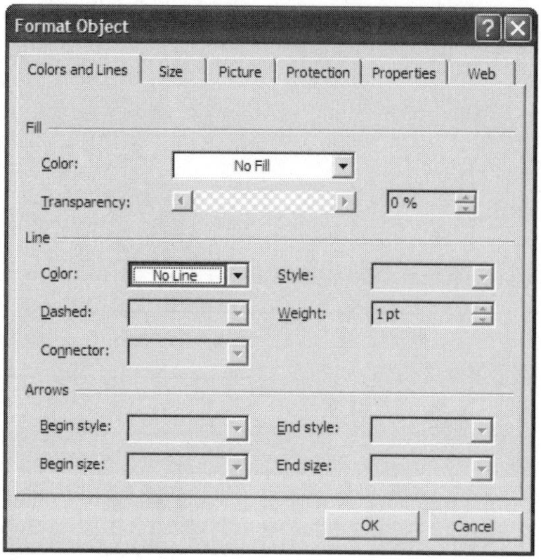

Figure 6-13 Easily format an ink area border.

The Format Object dialog box also controls how the ink area will respond as you insert, delete, and reformat cells. By default, ink areas move as you insert and delete cells, but they will not change size if you change the width of columns or rows. If you have an ink area that needs to stay in one place or an ink area where ink areas must remain aligned with specific cells, you can change this behavior on the Properties tab. Dramatic resizing can seriously reduce the readability of your ink, as shown in Figure 6-14.

If you password-protect your worksheet so that others can see the contents but cannot make changes, all of your ink areas are protected as well. The Protection tab in the Format Object dialog box lets you unprotect specific ink areas without unprotecting the spreadsheet cells. This lets users edit only existing ink areas, however, and not add new ones. If you want to protect your spreadsheet but let users edit and add ink areas, customize the protection to exclude objects. To customize protection, select Protection from the Tools menu and then select Protect Sheet. In the Protect Sheet dialog box, scroll down in the list of allowable actions and check Edit Objects, as shown in Figure 6-15. This is a nifty trick to let other tablet users use ink to comment on your spreadsheet without changing the spreadsheet itself.

Figure 6-14   If needed, ink areas can resize with changes to the size of columns and rows.

Figure 6-15   Checking Edit Objects allows users to add and edit comments on protected spreadsheets.

> **Note**   You cannot insert an ink area into an Excel comment as you can into a Word comment.

Using the Tablet Pack with PowerPoint

While creating slides in PowerPoint has always been easy, the Tablet Pack adds a whole new dimension. Now you can create slides by simply drawing them with the pen or by mixing ink areas with typed titles and pictures. Creating a slide with your pen is very useful when you are away from your office and need to make a new slide quickly, without the support of an art department or stock images. These slides also create a very different feel for your presentations, as demonstrated by Figure 6-16. Depending on your audience, you may choose slides containing your handwriting and drawings strictly for the effect.

Figure 6-16   Slides containing your handwriting and drawings create a very different feel for a presentation.

Creating a slide with one large ink area, as in Figure 6-16, is pretty simple. Insert an ink area onto a blank slide, resize it to fill the slide, and start drawing. Mixing text, pictures, and ink takes a little more planning. Suppose you had a picture that you wanted to annotate with hand-drawn text. If you create one ink area, even if it is behind the picture it will obscure the picture whenever you draw. Instead, create multiple ink areas for the individual elements, as shown in Figure 6-17. This not only allows you to see what you're doing, but also allows you to use custom animations in each ink area separately rather than having them all appear at once.

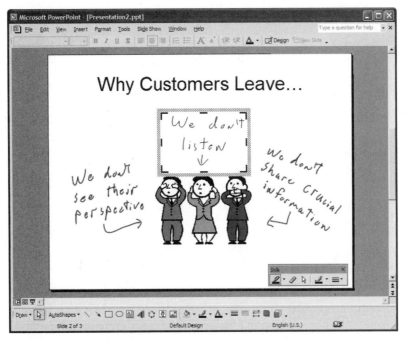

Figure 6-17   Use multiple ink areas to avoid obscuring pictures or other objects.

As in Word, you can add a border to an ink area in PowerPoint, but it always has solid white backgrounds. Because of this, you many need to use the Order commands on the Drawing toolbar or shortcut menu to bring pictures to the front of ink areas if they are getting cut off. Once you have the order perfect, protect the order by selecting all the objects and grouping them.

For even more control over your ink in PowerPoint, select the ink on the ink area, copy it, deselect the ink area, and then paste the ink into the presentation without inserting a new ink area. Just as with Word, this converts the ink into a picture that you can rotate and make transparent but can no longer edit.

Save as Picture

If you create a great slide that you want to convert into a picture, you can save the entire slide as an Enhanced Windows Metafile as was demonstrated in Chapter 4 for creating a Journal template. You can also save just some of the ink and other objects on a slide as a picture by selecting them, right-tapping on the selection, and selecting Save As Picture from the shortcut menu. This trick is handy if you want to use the ease of layout in PowerPoint to create a picture you will later use in Word. It's also helpful to use your slide or drawing in an application that isn't a part of Office.

Try This   Add your signature to a letter you create in Word by inserting an ink area and signing. Next sign your name in a PowerPoint ink area, and save the signature as a metafile picture. Insert the picture into your Word letter where you would normally sign. Both methods allow you to sign the letter, but the second technique saves you the trouble of creating a new ink area in every letter you create and works when you're using a keyboard and mouse instead of the pen. As an interesting side note, there's no legal precedent as to whether an ink signature is considered a legal signature or not. Given the ease of signing on the tablet, this may come up in the next few years.

Using Ink During Presentations

Marking up a slide with ink before a presentation is cool, but far more visually powerful is drawing on the slide during the presentation itself. This Tablet Pack feature offers an enormous increase in presentation interactivity. It works by adding several pen tools to the slide show shortcut menu available during a presentation. The full slide show shortcut menu is shown in Figure 6-18.

By default, the slide show shortcut menu can be displayed during a presentation by right-tapping or by tapping the slide show shortcut menu button. The display options for the slide show shortcut menu are controlled by selecting Options from the Tools menu and selecting the View tab, as shown in Figure 6-19.

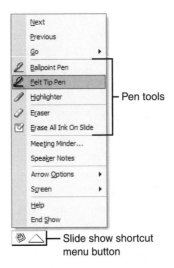

Pen tools

Slide show shortcut menu button

Figure 6-18   The slide show shortcut menu is available during presentations.

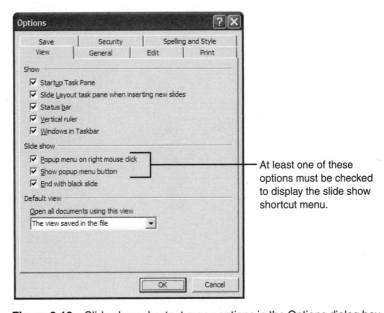

At least one of these options must be checked to display the slide show shortcut menu.

Figure 6-19   Slide show shortcut menu options in the Options dialog box.

Both ways of displaying the slide show shortcut menu are on by default. Some people prefer having only the slide show shortcut menu button so that they cannot accidentally open the shortcut menu by resting their pen on the screen too long. Other people find the slide show shortcut menu button distracting and prefer having it disabled.

When you select any of the pen tools, the entire screen becomes a transparent writing ink area. You must tap once with the pen somewhere on the screen before you can start writing or drawing. Once you do this, you can draw on any part of the slide you want. As shown in Figure 6-20, this lets you draw directly on pictures, something you cannot do with a normal ink area. While the pen tool is active, a simplified Ink toolbar is visible that allows you to change the ink color or return to the slide show by tapping the Arrow button. You must tap the Arrow button to return PowerPoint to normal operation or to change drawing tools. This takes a bit of practice, so be sure to try it out by yourself before using it in a presentation.

Figure 6-20   While a pen tool is active during a presentation, a simplified Ink toolbar is visible.

> **Tip**   Ensure that the Input Panel gesture to make Input Panel appear is turned off before using the pen tools during a presentation. If it isn't, Input Panel is likely to appear suddenly as you move your pen back and forth over the screen. The Input Panel gesture settings are available in the Tablet And Pen Settings control panel.

Saving Your Ink Annotations

When you finish marking up a slide, you can either erase all the ink with the Erase All Ink On Slide command from the slide show shortcut menu or leave it on the slide and return to the slide show. If you leave it on the slide, it will still be there if you return to the slide later in the presentation. If you end the slide show and there is still ink on any of your slides, you will be asked whether you want the ink to become a permanent part of your presentation, as shown in Figure 6-21. If you answer No, the ink will disappear. If you answer Yes, the ink will be converted into new, transparent ink areas.

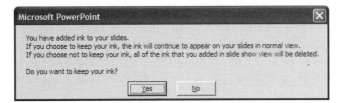

Figure 6-21   If you annotated your slide presentation with ink, you'll be asked whether you want to save your changes.

> **Tip**   If your audience members also have tablets, consider giving them a copy of your presentation beforehand and letting them take personal notes directly on their own slides.

While saving your ink annotations is a great feature, there are a couple of things to keep in mind if you use it:

- Transparent ink areas have more jagged ink. If you save the ink and then view the show again, the ink will not appear as smooth as when you first drew it.

■   Saved ink becomes part of the slide and cannot be edited or erased with pen tools during subsequent presentations.

If the jagged ink doesn't bother you, the save ink feature is a great workaround to create a transparent ink area that simply isn't an option when you author a slide. Build the slide with all the elements except the ink, view the show, add the additional ink you want, and save it.

Using the Tablet Pack with Outlook

During field trials of the tablet, one of the most positive responses people had was in how it allowed them to use their e-mail. One aspect of this was how comfortable and easy it was to quickly review and delete messages while waiting in an airport or sitting on the couch. The other component was how much people enjoyed jotting off a quick message in their own handwriting. Ink in e-mail creates a much more human, more informal effect and lets you include handwriting and drawings in your messages.

"There is an emotional reaction when people discover ink e-mail."
—Cynthia Tee, Tablet PC Team

For ink e-mail to work easily, you must use Word as your e-mail editor. While this is usually the default setting, you can check this setting in Outlook by selecting Options from the Tools menu. On the Mail Format tab, the Use Microsoft Word To Edit E-Mail Messages check box should be checked, as shown in Figure 6-22.

Figure 6-22   On the Mail Format tab, you can specify Word as your e-mail editor.

Since you are using Word to edit the e-mail, inserting an ink area into an e-mail message is identical to inserting ink into a Word document. Tap anywhere in the body of a new message, insert an ink area, and start drawing. When the recipient sees your e-mail, the ink will appear as an image inserted into your message. Most modern e-mail readers handle this quite well, but some do not. If you don't know whether the recipient uses an e-mail program that supports pictures, such as Outlook or Outlook Express, it's usually a good idea to include a short typed sentence asking them to tell you if they didn't see the handwritten part of the message. It's also a good idea not to use complex formatting of ink objects in an e-mail. It might look cool before you send it, but results are somewhat unpredictable. As shown in Figure 6-23, you can use ink in replies as well as in new messages When a message containing ink is forwarded or replied to, the ink may or may not remain visible. The ink area might appear as the text "<<object>>" in further messages. If your message is more important than a quick and informal note, you might want to type it rather than write it in ink.

Figure 6-23   You can put ink into new messages or replies, but it's usually best to keep the formatting simple.

> **Tip**   If you just want to put a small bit of ink, such as a smiling face, into an e-mail that you are typing or writing with Input Panel, you can do it without inserting an ink area. Draw it on the Input Panel writing pad, and then send it as ink to your e-mail.

If you do not want to use Word as your e-mail editor, you can still insert an ink area into your messages. First go to the Mail Format tab on the Options dialog box, and uncheck the settings to use Word as your e-mail editor. While you are there, change the Compose In This Message Format drop-down list to Rich Text. Tap in the body of a new message where you want the ink to go, and select Object from the Insert menu. The Insert Object dialog box, shown in Figure 6-24, lists all the objects that Office can create. Select the Ink Drawing And Writing object type, and tap OK. The ink area will appear in the body of the message.

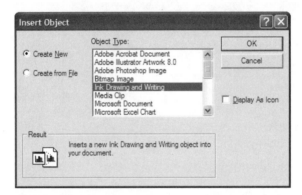

Figure 6-24   You don't have to use Word as your e-mail editor, and you can insert ink areas into rich text messages.

Messages must be in rich text format for the Insert Object command to be available. This becomes an issue when someone sends you a message in one of the other two common e-mail formats, HTML and plain text. Since Outlook replies in the same format the message was sent, the Insert Object command will not be an option unless you change the format of your message to rich text. With Word as your e-mail editor, you can insert ink in messages of any format; however, only rich text and HTML e-mails support pictures. If you try to send a reply containing ink in plain text format, you will be given the option of converting the message to HTML or discarding your ink pictures, as shown in Figure 6-25.

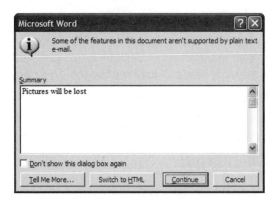

Figure 6-25   Dialog box that appears if you try to send a reply with pictures in plain text format.

You can insert ink areas in e-mail messages, and you can also insert ink areas in other Outlook items, such as tasks, appointments, contacts, journal entries, and meeting requests. In fact, the only place you can't put an ink area in Outlook is in a note. Keeping a handwritten message or drawing, such as a map, together with its corresponding appointment or task in Outlook is a great feature. Figure 6-26 shows a ink area in an Outlook task.

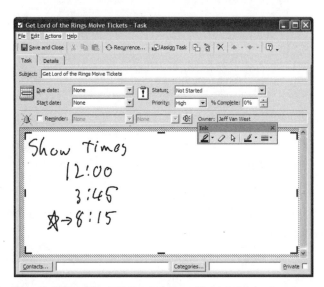

Figure 6-26   Most Outlook items will accept ink when you use the Insert Object command and select the Ink Writing And Drawing type.

> **Note**   You have to tap an ink area only once to edit it in Word, Excel, or PowerPoint. To edit an ink area in an Outlook item, you must tap it twice. The exception is ink areas in e-mail messages if you are using Word as your e-mail editor.

Using the Tablet Pack with Journal

Tablet Pack adds a few features to Journal that let you convert handwriting directly to Outlook items. After Tablet Pack is installed, the Convert Selection To E-mail option on the Actions menu is replaced by a Convert Selection To command with a submenu. The submenu contains the e-mail option and adds options to create new appointments, contacts, or tasks using your handwriting, as shown in Figure 6-27.

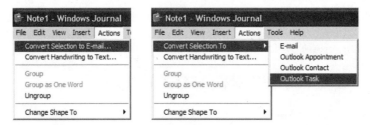

Figure 6-27   Convert Selection To commands that appear when the Tablet Pack is installed.

The new convert functions provide a quick way for you to take those details and to-dos you jot down in your notes and put them into your daily organizer so that they actually get done. To create the new Outlook item, first select the handwriting you want converted and choose the target Outlook item from the Actions menu. The Convert Selection To commands are also available directly from the shortcut menu if you enabled Show Extended Shortcut Menus in Journal Options, as shown in Figure 6-28.

> **Note**   Outlook does not need to be running for the Convert Selection To commands to work.

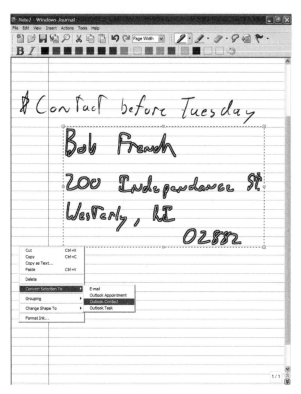

Figure 6-28   Converting a selection to an Outlook contact.

When you select a Convert Selection To command, a Convert dialog box appears with the converted text, as shown in Figure 6-29. You can correct any errors in the converted text while still viewing the original ink. An alternative list of words is also available.

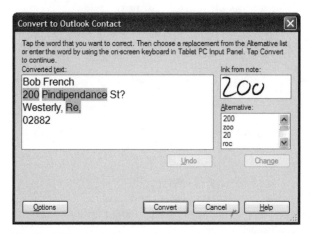

Figure 6-29   The Convert dialog box allows you to correct the converted text.

Once the text is correct and you tap Convert, a new Outlook item will open. If the item is an appointment or a contact, the text appears in the body section so that you can select and drag the appropriate information into the appropriate fields. If it is a task, the converted text goes directly into the subject field. Figure 6-30 shows the converted text in an Outlook contact.

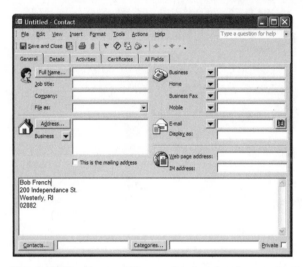

Figure 6-30 Here are the results of converting a selection to an Outlook contact.

Because tasks have the text put directly into the subject field, the text won't appear correctly if the original handwriting covers two lines. If this happens, tap the Options button on the Convert dialog box and uncheck Preserve Line Breaks From Notes. All the task text now appears on one line. This is especially useful when you employ some creative lasso work to select exactly the text you want inserted into Outlook, as shown in Figure 6-31.

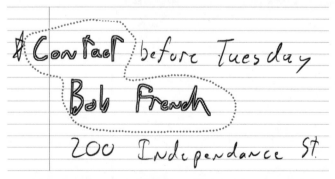

Figure 6-31 When converting a multi-line selection to an Outlook task, you'll want to remove line breaks.

Inserting Meeting Information from Outlook

Tablet Pack lets Journal take meeting information from Outlook and insert it into a Journal note. This is a quick way to add the date, time, place, people, and subject of a meeting right into your notes for future reference. To add the meeting information, select Outlook Meeting Information from the Insert menu in Journal. When the Insert Meeting Information dialog box appears, as shown in Figure 6-32, select the date and the meeting and tap OK.

Figure 6-32   Select the Outlook meeting information to insert into a Journal note.

The meeting information appears in a new text box in your note as shown in Figure 6-33.

> **Tip**   If you save your new note after inserting the meeting information and before writing anything, the filename for the new note will be the word "Subject" plus the subject of your meeting. You may want to position the text box so that the "Subject" line is in the note title area of the note for clarity as well.

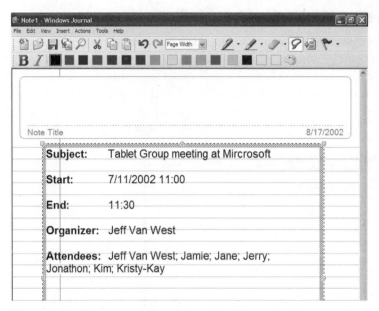

Figure 6-33 You can quickly add meeting information into your Journal notes directly from Outlook.

Key Points

- Tablet Pack lets you add ink directly into Word 2002, Excel 2002, PowerPoint 2002, and Outlook 2002 in ink areas.

- Tablet Pack works only with Office XP on a tablet, but the ink is visible by most versions of Office and most e-mail viewers.

- The results of copy and paste and the options for formatting ink areas vary depending on how they are selected.

- Ink areas always have solid white backgrounds except in Excel and when created during a PowerPoint slide show.

- Pen tools are available during PowerPoint presentations from the slide show shortcut menu.

- Tablet Pack adds conduits for easier exchange of information between Journal and Outlook.

Part III

More Muscle for Your Tablet

"Mobility is a personal thing. For some people it just means going down the hall. For others it's going halfway around the world."
—Jim Cox, Windows XP Tablet PC Edition team

7

Networking and Traveling with Your Tablet

The expressed goal of the Tablet PC team was getting people to use their computers in places and situations they never used them before. How you will adapt your tablet to your work style is strictly personal. The first part of this chapter describes how you can use your tablet offline and how you can connect to different networks. The latter part of this chapter relates some of my experiences using my tablet on a coast-to-coast work trip and describes some of the benefits and challenges. Whether you plan to travel around the office or around the globe, all tablet users should understand the ins and outs of connecting to local networks and the Internet. If the Tablet PC team meets its goal of enabling you to take your tablet places you never took your computer before, connecting and disconnecting to networks will be a daily activity.

"Mobility is a personal thing. For some people it just means going down the hall. For others it's going halfway around the world."
        —*Jim Cox, Windows XP Tablet PC Edition team.*

Working On and Off Networks

Having a computer as portable as the tablet doesn't do you any good if your files don't come with you. Because much of the information that you work with yourself or share with others is stored on a network, easily working on, off, and between networks is central to having a satisfying experience with your tablet.

In the following sections, I'll briefly cover how to work with network files and folders on your computer when you're offlineoffline and still keep the information in sync, how to maintain Web pages for offline reference, and how to set up your e-mail client so that you can read and respond to messages when you're not connected to your e-mail server. I'll also provide some background on working with a virtual private network and wireless networks. Although the information presented here isn't unique to working with a tablet, setting up your tablet for optimal mobility lets you use it most effectively.

Offline Folders and Files

To work with your files when you're traveling or otherwise unable to connect to a network, you need a copy of them physically stored on your tablet. Using Windows XP, you can designate a folder or a file that's stored on a network server to be available offline. Windows then creates a folder on your local hard drive in which it stores copies of the files. When you connect to the network again, Windows synchronizes the local copy with the version on the network, providing you the means to resolve conflicts should they arise.

> **Glossary**   *Synchronization* is the process of making the files in two different locations identical.

Setting Up Offline Files

Before you assign a particular folder or file to be available offline, you need to configure your computer to work with offline files. If your computer is part of a workgroup rather than part of a domain, you can't set up a file or folder for offline use until you have turned off Fast User Switching, the feature in Windows XP that permits more than one person to be logged on to a single computer at the same time. To be sure that Fast User Switching isn't enabled, open User Accounts in Control Panel and then tap Change The Way Users Log On Or Off. Uncheck the Use Fast User Switching option, and then tap Apply Options.

> **Glossary**   In Windows, a *workgroup* is a group of networked computers with no central administration services. Small office or home networks are usually workgroups.

Glossary   In Windows, a *domain* is a group of networked computers that are centrally administered. Domains are more powerful and secure but are also more complicated and require some expertise to manage. Large office networks are usually domains. When you log into a computer that is part of a domain, the login dialog box includes a list to select the domain.

To set up offline files, open Folder Options in Control Panel (Folder Options is under Appearance And Themes if you display Control Panel in Category View) and then tap the Offline Files tab, shown in Figure 7-1.

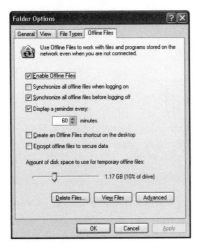

Figure 7-1   Set up options for handling your offline files on the Offline Files tab.

Before setting any other option, check Enable Offline Files. With offline files enabled, you can decide when you want to synchronize. The default option will synchronize your files before logging off. You can also synchronize when logging on or be reminded that you need to synchronize your offline files before logging back on. The important thing to remember is that those files need to be synchronized on a regular basis.

Other options on this tab include creating a shortcut on your desktop to your offline files and encrypting the data in offline folders for additional security. If you feel the need for such security, get more information about the ins and outs of encryption before proceeding.

Designating Offline Files

To designate a file or a folder to be available offline, you must first connect to the network from your tablet. Using My Computer or My Network Places, open the network share that contains the files you want to work with offline. Right-tap on either the folder icon or a particular file you want, and then choose Make Available Offline from the shortcut menu.

Choosing this command starts the Offline Files Wizard, which, as you tap through its screens, presents many of the options included on the Offline Files tab of the Folder Options control panel. If a folder you've marked for offline use includes subfolders, you'll see the dialog box shown in Figure 7-2 when you tap Finish. Select whichever option best fits your needs.

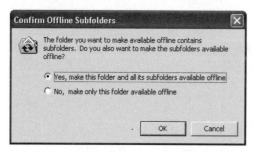

Figure 7-2   When you make a folder that contains subfolders available offline, you can decide whether to include the subfolders.

> **Tip**   The file server doesn't need to be anything fancy. I keep all my work on my old desktop machine running Windows XP Professional and keep synchronized copies on my tablet. Whichever computer I use, I always have my files available and up-to-date.

> **Tip**   A great way to back up the work on your tablet is to set your My Documents folder on the tablet to point to a folder on the network and then make it available offline. To change the target of your My Documents folder, right-tap on My Documents in the Start menu and select Properties from the shortcut menu. On the Target tab, enter the path to the folder on the server.

Synchronizing Files

In most cases, synchronization is straightforward. For example, if you modify an offline document on your computer and the copy on the network was not changed, the network copy is updated with the copy from your local offline folder. Similarly, if the copy on the network has changed and your local copy has not, the local copy is updated during synchronization. If both copies have been changed, you'll see the Resolve File Conflicts dialog box, shown in Figure 7-3. As you can see, you can elect to keep one version or the other or both.

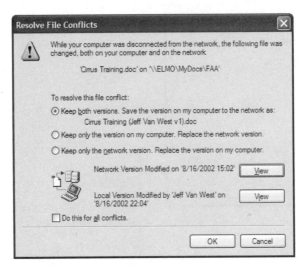

Figure 7-3   Use the Resolve File Conflicts dialog box to determine which version of a file to keep when file conflicts occur during synchronization.

Other synchronization logic is followed if you delete a file from your local offline files folder or a file has been deleted from the network. As long as a file hasn't changed, if you delete the file from your computer, it's deleted from the network when the two locations are synchronized. The same pattern is followed if the file was first deleted from the network. If a file is deleted in one location but has been changed in the other, Windows displays a dialog box that lets you sort through whether to retain the version that's still stored or delete it.

Manual Synchronization

You can synchronize your offline files any time you're connected to the network by right-tapping the folder or file you want synchronized and selecting Synchronize from the shortcut menu. You can synchronize all your offline folders at once in Windows Explorer by tapping Synchronize on the Tools menu. Tapping this command displays the Items To Synchronize dialog box shown in Figure 7-4.

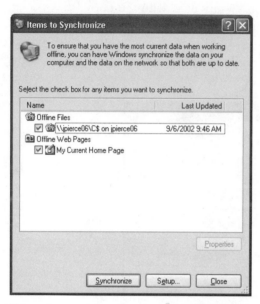

Figure 7-4   Use the Items To Synchronize dialog box to synchronize all your offline files.

The Items To Synchronize dialog box allows you to select the items to synchronize and to specify synchronization settings. If you tap the Setup button, you can specify when synchronization should occur and other settings. The Properties button displays the files that will be synchronized.

In the Items To Synchronize dialog box, uncheck any of the items that you don't want synchronized and then tap the Synchronize button. With the details pane shown, you'll see a progress dialog box such as that shown in Figure 7-5.

> **Caution**   When you're connected to the network and working with your offline files, the files on your tablet will be synchronized when you save your work. If you leave the network without saving or synchronizing, either manually or automatically, your work might not be saved on the tablet.

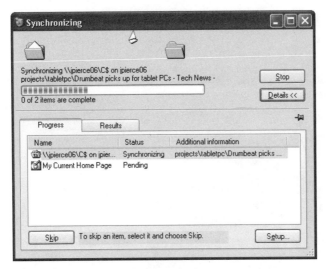

Figure 7-5   Synchronization in progress.

Tip   If you work on a large office network, another option for offline file access is a roaming user profile. This will not only keep a copy of files and settings on your tablet but also make your files, and your entire desktop, available from virtually any computer in your office. For more information about roaming profiles, search Help And Support on the Start menu and ask your network administrator.

Offline Web Pages

The Web pages or sites that you often refer to can also be made available for use offline. You can visit the site and obtain information from it without being connected to the Internet. Think of the advantages of reading through your favorite online periodical on a long coast-to-coast flight.

A Web page that you want to view offline must be included in your list of favorites in Internet Explorer. For sites already among your favorites, right-tap the favorite entry on the Favorites menu and then tap Make Available Offline on the shortcut menu. The Add Favorite dialog box, shown in Figure 7-6, includes the Make Available Offline check box for a Web page you're adding as a new favorite.

Figure 7-6 You can select the Make Available Offline option when you add a Web page to your list of favorites.

You can tailor the offline behavior of a favorite Web page by tapping the Customize button in the Add Favorite dialog box, which starts the Offline Favorite Wizard. In the first page of the Offline Favorite Wizard, shown in Figure 7-7, you establish the level to which material linked to the offline page will also be available offline. You can download only the page you've marked as a favorite or as many as three levels beyond that page. In other words, you can download the page marked as a favorite (zero levels), the pages that page is linked to (one level), the pages those pages are linked to (two levels), and the pages linked to those (three levels). The number of links and amount of data at three levels will be significant, and the time required to download all those pages is considerable. Downloading even two levels deep captures more content than you might expect. Be cautious about turning this setting up beyond the first level.

For further control of how an offline Web page is downloaded, right-tap the favorite entry on the Favorites menu and then tap Properties on the shortcut menu. The Download tab provides much of the information captured by the Offline Favorite Wizard, as shown in Figure 7-8.

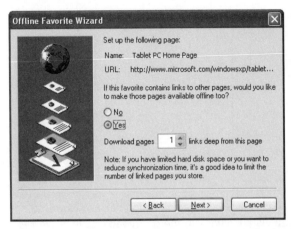

Figure 7-7   Downloading more than one level of links deep can take a lot of time.

Figure 7-8   Settings for downloading offline Web pages can be specified on the Download tab of the Properties dialog box.

Tapping the Advanced button on the Download tab lets you select whether to download images, sound and video, and ActiveX controls and Java applets, as shown in Figure 7-9. You can also select whether you want to download links to only HTML pages. I usually check all the options in the Items To Download On Pages area and uncheck the Only To HTML Pages check box to download all links because it is a pain to discover some key item is missing as your airplane is leveling off at 32,000 feet.

Figure 7-9   The Advanced Download Options dialog box allows you to specify what content you want included in the download of offline Web pages.

Offline E-Mail

As you can with files and Web pages, you can set up your e-mail accounts so that you have access to messages you want to read or respond to offline. There are two ways to work with e-mail offline: offline folders and remote mail.

> **Note**   Most of the steps discussed here assume that your e-mail client is Microsoft Outlook 2002 and your e-mail server is Microsoft Exchange. Other e-mail clients have similar capabilities. Check the product documentation for detailed information.

> **Note**   This discussion of offline e-mail is just an introduction to get you started. For additional information on using offline e-mail in Outlook, consult the Outlook Help or the book *Microsoft Outlook Version 2002 Inside Out* (Microsoft Press, 2001).

Offline Folders

Offline folders allow you to have access to Outlook folders and Outlook items (such as calendar, contacts, tasks, and notes) offline and then synchronize your offline and online item stores when you connect to your e-mail server again. To use offline folders, you first need to have an offline folder file, and then you can perform the synchronization process.

To create an offline folder file for offline e-mail, follow these steps:

1. Open Outlook 2002.

2. On the Tools menu, tap E-Mail Accounts.

3. Under the E-Mail label, select View Or Change Existing E-Mail Accounts and then tap Next to see the list of existing e-mail accounts.

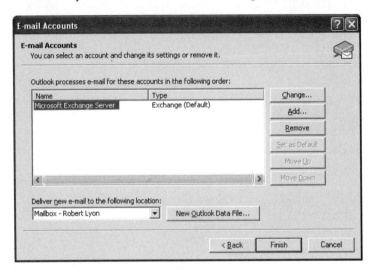

4. Tap the Change button, tap More Settings, tap the Advanced tab, and then tap Offline Folder Settings to see the Offline Folder File Settings dialog box.

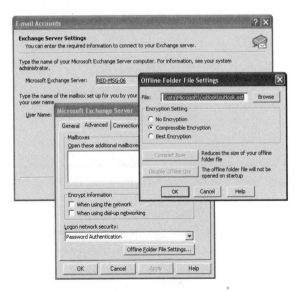

In this dialog box, Outlook displays the path to a default offline folder file (Documents and Settings***<username>***\Local Settings\Application Data\Microsoft\Outlook\Outlook.ost). The offline folder file (.ost) stores a copy of the Outlook folders and items in your mailbox that have been identified as available offline, although you will not see a duplicate set of folders and items displayed in Outlook. Tap OK, and if a dialog box appears asking whether you want to create the file, tap Yes. This file will be associated with your e-mail account.

Once you have created an offline folder file, you can specify which items you want to be available offline. In Outlook, this is accomplished with send/receive groups. To edit the default All Accounts group, tap Tools, Send/Receive Settings, Define Send/Receive Groups to display the Send/Receive Groups dialog box. Select the All Accounts group, and tap Edit. In the Send/Receive Settings dialog box shown in Figure 7-10, you can specify which items to include in the group.

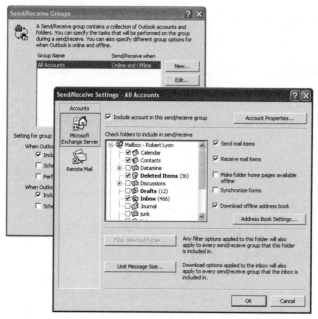

Figure 7-10   Specify which items to include in the send/receive group.

Before you can work offline in Outlook, you need to synchronize the offline folder file with your mailbox on the e-mail server. To manually synchronize your offline folders, choose Tools, Send/Receive, and then tap Send And

Receive All to synchronize all folders or tap the send/receive group name (such as All Accounts) to synchronize the items in that group. Figure 7-11 shows a sample of the Outlook Send/Receive Progress dialog box that is displayed.

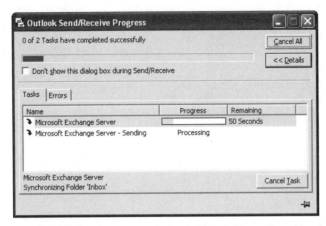

Figure 7-11   Synchronize the offline folders file with an Exchange mailbox.

After you've performed this synchronization, you can work with your e-mail offline and then synchronize your offline work with your mailbox on the server the next time you connect to the network. Messages you've composed offline will be sent to their recipients, and changes to your Outlook items (calendar, contacts, tasks, and notes) are updated.

How you switch between working offline and on line depends on your e-mail account type. If you're using Post Office Protocol 3 (POP3), Internet Message Access Protocol (IMAP), or HTML e-mail, select Work Offline from the File menu. If you're using Exchange Server, the General tab in the properties dialog box for your Exchange Server e-mail account includes several options for automatically and manually connecting when you start Outlook, as shown in Figure 7-12. When using Exchange Server, you'll have to restart Outlook to switch between working offline and on line.

> **Tip**   Choose to work offline when you carry your tablet out of wireless network range to prevent a barrage of annoying "Unable to Connect to Server" messages.

Figure 7-12   Options for switching between working offline and on line when using Exchange Server.

Remote Mail

Another method for managing e-mail while you're on the road or otherwise away from the network is remote mail. Remote mail has the benefit of letting you identify which e-mail messages you want to read and respond to without having to download all your messages. Instead, when you dial in or connect in some other way to your e-mail server—perhaps over a long-distance call—you can download message headers, skipping the contents of the message bodies, and then disconnect from the server. Free from a potentially expensive or slow connection, you can sort and review the message headers, deciding which messages to download completely, which to keep on the server, and which you can simply delete at this point. You then connect to the server again to process the messages as you indicated. However, unlike offline folders, remote mail works only with messages in your Inbox.

> **Tip**   Avoiding the costly and time-consuming download of large file attachments over a dial-up connection is reason enough for using remote mail.

Remote mail requires that you've set up an offline folder file in Outlook (see the previous section for the steps required to do this) or have set up Outlook to deliver e-mail messages to personal folders. After connecting to your server, download message headers by tapping Tools, Send/Receive, Work With Headers.

Remote mail is available for Exchange Server accounts only, but there are comparable features for other e-mail account types, such as POP3 and IMAP. If your e-mail account uses POP3, you can set up your account to download only message headers and select which messages you want moved from the server to your computer, which you want downloaded while retaining a copy on the server, and which you want to delete without downloading. You can also set a limit on the size of the messages to download. With an IMAP e-mail account, simply turning off the preview pane and AutoPreview lets you see and edit message headers without downloading the entire message.

Virtual Private Networks

A virtual private network (VPN) lets you use the Internet as a secure path to your organization's network. You can also set up a VPN to your home if you have a full-time Internet connection or phone line. VPNs are especially useful when you're traveling because you can connect to your office network from any Internet connection anywhere in the world. The data that's transmitted over the Internet is encrypted when it's sent between the computers defining the private network.

Setting up a VPN is beyond the scope of this book, and if your office network allows VPN access, you'll need the connection settings and passwords from your network administrator to set it up. My point in bringing it up here is both to let you know these connections exist and may be available at your company and to point out how VPNs can work around a Catch-22 of networks. Both VPNs and corporate networks are usually part of a domain, while home networks are usually workgroups. Your user profile on the tablet can log into a domain or a workgroup but not both. The situation comes up when you take your tablet that logs into a domain at work or for VPN access and try to log on to your home (workgroup) network, and you can't do it. There is no good solution for this, but two workarounds are to have all your home computers connect to the domain via VPNs, which is only possible if you have a broadband Internet connection, or to create two user profiles for your tablet that share a My Documents folder. You would use the workgroup profile to use your home network and the domain profile to use the VPN or the office network.

Wireless Networks

Your tablet was practically built for wireless networks. On a wireless network, you can walk from your office to a conference room and always have access to data on the network. Moreover, some airports, conference centers, and even coffee shops have installed wireless networks so that their patrons can connect to the Internet. Most wireless networks follow the IEEE 802.11b standard, also known as Wi-Fi, have a range of 50 to 300 feet, and can transmit data at up to 11 megabits per second. That's about one-tenth the speed of the average wired network but about ten times the speed of most broadband Internet connections. In other words, wireless may seem a bit slow transferring network files but Internet access will probably seem quite speedy.

> **Caution**   If you're working on line and walk out of network range, the network file you have open may close unexpectedly or cause an error. Be careful about dropping off a wireless network with network files open.

The wireless network connector on your tablet is communicating with a base station that broadcasts the network's presence, manages the transmission and reception of data, and provides a check point for secure access. Security for wireless computers can be achieved by using Wireless Equivalent Privacy (WEP). WEP protects data transmissions using a string of information called a key. There are shorter (40-bit) keys and longer (104-bit) keys, but the important distinction for you to know is between open and shared keys. An open key is used for public networks, such as in a coffee shop, where any computer can connect to the network. This key encrypts your transmissions to the base station, so the guy at the next table can't spy on your work, but anyone can join the network without permission. A shared key is a single password-like code that you must know to join the network. If you are prompted for a password when you try to connect to a wireless network it has a shared key. Shared keys are more secure than open keys, so long as the key itself remains secret. Most hardware that supports WEP uses a single key that's shared by the network's components. Shared keys should be changed frequently to hinder intruders from discovering them.

The support for wireless networks built into Windows XP automatically detects and connects to accessible networks within range. This feature is known as *wireless zero configuration*. As you use your tablet, Windows XP will build a list of the wireless networks you use and their settings. Automatic wireless network configuration will detect which network is available and adjust your network settings appropriately. You can configure Windows to try to connect to these various networks in the order in which you prefer by tapping the buttons to the right of the Preferred Networks list in the Wireless Network Connection Properties dialog box shown in Figure 7-13.

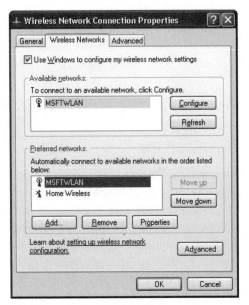

Figure 7-13   Setting the properties for your wireless connection.

> **Note**   For more information about wireless network setup and secu-
> rity, see *Microsoft Windows Security Inside Out for Windows XP and
> Windows 2000* (Microsoft Press, 2002).

Troubleshooting Wireless Networks

Like everything else with computers, wireless networks don't work perfectly all
the time. If you have trouble connecting to a wireless network, check to be sure
that Windows is set up for automatic configuration. Open the Wireless Network
Connection Properties dialog box for your wireless connection, and confirm
that the option Use Windows To Configure My Wireless Network Settings is
checked. Also check whether the Wireless Zero Configuration service is running on your computer. Do this by displaying the list of services (double-tap
Services in the Administrative Tools folder in Control Panel) and checking
whether the Status column shows that the Wireless Zero Configuration service
is running. You should start the service if it's not running. Sometimes switching
to the wired network and then back to the wireless one will reset the network
settings and fix a problem. Plaster walls in old homes and buildings can interfere with wireless network signals. If you're having trouble getting a good sig-
nal through walls in an old building, this might be the problem.

There is an additional level of network authentication with wireless networks that is controlled on the Advanced tab of the Wireless Network Connection Properties dialog box for a given wireless network. Normally this option can be left untouched, but if you have the problem of your tablet joining a network and then immediately dropping back off, try disabling this level of authentication. This problem is most common with home wireless-network base stations.

Try This   An ad-hoc wireless network lets two computers communicate directly with each other without any cables and without setting up a workgroup or a domain. This is a great way to exchange large files between two wireless-capable computers. To set up an ad-hoc wireless network, open the Network Connections control panel and double-tap your wireless network device. In the Wireless Network Connection Status dialog box, tap the Properties button on the General tab to open the Wireless Network Connection Properties dialog box. To add your own ad-hoc network, tap the Wireless Networks tab and then tap the Add button. Give the network a name, and check the option for a computer-to-computer (ad-hoc) network. When you tap OK, your computer should start broadcasting its availability for connection. On the other computer, double-tap the wireless network device in the Network Connections control panel. The network you just created should be available. It may take some experimenting with different WEP, authentication, and key settings to get everything connected, but once you get it working, it's really cool. Of course, whenever you connect to someone else's computer and exchange files, be sure your anti-virus software is running and up-to-date.

Login and Password Management

As you travel from network to network and place to place with your tablet, you will be logging in and being authenticated all the time. The login and password management tools used by Windows XP are not unique to the tablet, but because it's such a mobile computer, they deserve a brief mention here. For more information on login and password management, see the book, *Microsoft Windows XP Inside Out* (Microsoft Press, 2001).

The User Accounts control panel is the tool you use to manage your login and passwords. This control panel lets you control all the user passwords for your tablet, manage your .NET Passport and network passwords, and control what a user must do to log on to your tablet. The view of the User Accounts control panel is different depending on whether your tablet is part of a domain. Each view has essentially the same capabilities, but the steps to perform different operations and the location of options are different. Figure 7-14 and Figure 7-15 show the User Accounts control panel when your tablet is not part of a domain and when your tablet is part of a domain.

Figure 7-14   User Accounts control panel when tablet *is not* part of a domain.

Figure 7-15   User Accounts control panel when tablet *is* part of a domain.

There are two login and password features worth looking at. One is the .NET Passport built into Windows XP, and the other is network password management. Both features can be accessed by opening your user account in the User Accounts control panel.

.NET Passport

.NET Passport allows you to add a passport to a user account and then use that secure login to access hundreds of .NET Passport–enabled services and Web sites without having to log in over and over again. .NET Passport also lets you use the Windows Messenger service that is linked with Outlook in Office XP. Windows XP will probably launch the .NET Passport Wizard shown in Figure 7-16 automatically, but if it does not, or if you want to edit your account, you can access it through the User Accounts control panel.

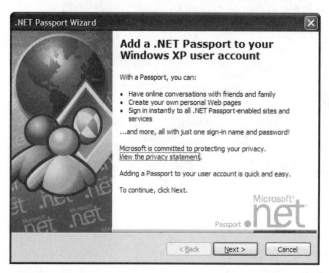

Figure 7-16   The .NET Passport Wizard lets you add a .NET Passport to your account.

Note   .NET Passport uses your e-mail address as your login name and a password of your choosing. While .NET is quite secure, it's still a good idea to use a different password than you use to log in to your corporate network.

Managing Network Passwords

When you log on to remote networks, you are often asked for a username and password. Entering these on the tablet can be a real pain without a keyboard available. Windows XP can save the login information and enter it for you, but the settings can be hard to find. Once you open your user account in the User Accounts control panel, tapping the Manage My Network Passwords option (or Manage Passwords button if your tablet is part of a domain) opens the Stored User Names And Passwords dialog box. Editing or creating an entry opens the Logon Information Properties dialog box shown in Figure 7-17. In this dialog box, you can specify the server you are logging in to, your username on that server, and your password. Once you have entered the information, Windows XP will enter the login automatically whenever you access that server.

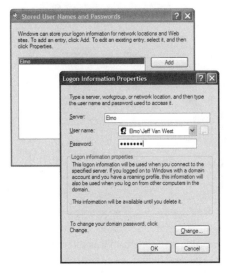

Figure 7-17   Saving your login information allows you to log in automatically to resources.

The disadvantage of automatic login is that anyone with access to your tablet can now log in from your user account. To protect your user account, you should set up your tablet so that users must log in with a username and password when the tablet starts up and potentially when it resumes from standby and hibernate. Setting up your tablet so that it requires a password when resuming from standby is discussed in the "Security Concerns" section later in this chapter.

If your tablet is not part of a domain, the easiest way to access all your login and password options at once is to open the Run dialog box from the Start menu, type **control userpasswords2** in the Open box, and press Enter. The alternative User Accounts control panel shown in Figure 7-18 appears, which is essentially the User Accounts control panel displayed when your tablet is part of a domain.

> **Tip**   For logon security, make sure the Users Must Enter A User Name And Password To Use This Computer check box (when tablet is not part of a domain) and the Require Users To Press Ctrl+Alt+Delete (tablet security button) check box are checked.

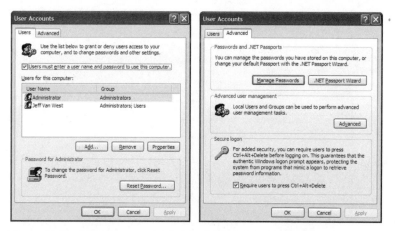

Figure 7-18   The Users and Advanced tabs of the User Accounts control panel. If your tablet is not part of a domain, you can open this alternative control panel by using the **control userpasswords2** command.

Five Thousand Miles with a Tablet

During the course of writing this book, I took the tablet on a business trip from Seattle, Washington, to Providence, Rhode Island, to Columbus, Ohio, and back to Seattle. Before the trip, I was pretty enamored with the tablet. After the trip, I was in love. The physical form of the tablet made it so much easier to use away from my desk that I ended up using it in places I just couldn't use a normal computer, such as standing in line at the airport. Mobility is a personal thing, but here are a few of my insights from my travels.

Backup and Security Plans

All portable computers have one inherent risk: your data is very vulnerable. The computer can be stolen, dropped, forgotten, or damaged as you travel. Even if the computer is fine, the data on hard drives is susceptible to strong magnetic fields and sudden shocks. If you're going to travel a fair amount with your tablet, you should consider an on-the-road backup solution. Even if you have a normal backup plan, a complete backup of your work that's still at home or on an office server that you can't access is virtually useless. The on-the-road backup need not be a complete backup of everything on your computer because having the ability to reinstall Office on a tablet that was stolen doesn't help much. What you want is a backup of your critical files—usually part or all of your My Documents folder and perhaps your Outlook files—that you can continue to update as you travel and that you can retrieve files from in an emergency. Because these files occupy only a fraction of your hard drive, you have several options for backup devices.

Portable Backup Devices

Following is a list of some portable backup devices that you could use to store your data files.

- **Removable Media**   Writable CDs, Iomega Zip, and other drives work well for large amounts of data, but they aren't the best thing for the road. They require you to carry both the media drive and blank CDs or discs and usually require their own power supply. If your computer is gone and you need to use a rented machine, sometimes these drives will work immediately and sometimes they require special software to be installed.

- **USB and FireWire Hard Drives**   These are portable drives capable of lightning-fast transfer rates for huge quantities of data, over 100 GB in some cases. They usually weigh a pound or less and draw their power from the computer or from their own rechargeable batteries. These drives work on most modern computers without installing special software as well. If you have a lot of data you need available by backup, such as large audio or video files, these drives are a good solution.

Tip   Want a FireWire hard drive for backups that also plays tunes and functions as a PDA? Apple's iPod works with Windows, too.

- **USB Pen Drives**   If your work is mostly text and a few PowerPoint presentations that don't take up much space, it will probably fit on a pen drive. These drives are about the size of a fat highlighter and can fit on a keychain, weigh only an ounce or two, don't require a power supply, and have no moving parts to break. They also work on virtually any modern computer without any special software. They don't hold nearly as much data as a USB or FireWire hard drives, but for many people they offer the easiest and most portable backup solution. Since most of my work was in Word, PowerPoint, and Windows Journal, I backed up to a 256-MB pen drive on my trip.

- **Internet Backup**   Backing up over the Internet has the advantage that it requires no additional hardware and can't be stolen, but it does require an Internet connection and either remote access to your company server or an account with one of the Internet backup services. Internet backups are also slower and less readily accessible in an emergency than hard drives in your physical possession.

- **PDA Backup**   Your PDA or cell phone calendar and address book can be a useful part of your backup solution. Because I synchronize Outlook with my PDA and leave copies of my e-mail messages on my e-mail server, I never back up my Outlook files on the road.

Backup vs. Synchronization Software

Most backup solutions, including the Windows Backup utility, create one large backup file containing all the selected files on your hard drive. Figure 7-19 shows Windows Backup in advanced mode. Windows Backup is accessible from Programs\Accessories\System Tools\Backup.

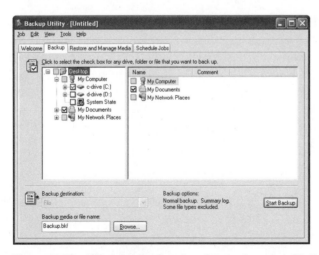

Figure 7-19   Windows Backup in advanced mode with the My Documents folder selected for backup.

This is a space-efficient way to back up, but it isn't what you want on the road because retrieving your files requires the software that created the backup (which was probably lost with your damaged or missing computer) and a lot of time. This is not the situation you want to find yourself in five minutes before your presentation starts! Instead, use a synchronization program that maintains a complete copy of your files the same way offline file access does as described earlier in this chapter. This way you can simply plug in your backup media to another computer and immediately access any of your files without any delays.

There's a saying among system administrators that having only one backup is almost as bad as having no backups. In the unlikely event that something happens while you're creating a backup, you could lose both files. If you want some extra security, back up to more than one folder. Figure 7-20 shows my backup system for this book, in which I synchronized files with different directories depending on the day of the week. This also allowed me to go back a few days to look at an old version of a file if I needed it. Once you have a backup system, find a time to use it that best fits your work habits or program the software to prompt you to back up on a specific schedule. Synchromagic by Gelosoft *(http://www.gelosoft.com)* is a great and inexpensive synchronization and backup application that works well under Windows XP and provides plenty of options for backup style and scheduling.

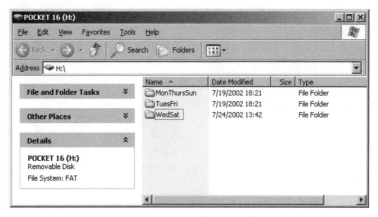

Figure 7-20 Your on-the-road backup solution should back up individual files rather than create one large backup file. You may also want to back up to more than one folder.

Tip Keep a copy of your synchronization software installer and registration number on your backup drive. If you use a loaner computer for an extended period while yours is unavailable, you will be able to continue using your backup regimen.

Backing Up Outlook Data Files

If you use Outlook at your company, then all of your Outlook information is backed up on the company server. If you synchronize it with a PDA, then your e-mail is not backed up, but the synchronized calendar, contacts, tasks, and notes are. If you don't fall into one of these categories, or you want to keep a backup of your Outlook data with you, you need to find the folder containing your Outlook data files and add them to your backup. To see the data files used by Outlook, tap Data File Management on the File menu to see the Outlook Data Files dialog box. Next select one of the files listed (in many cases there is only one) and tap Settings. The dialog box that appears contains the location of the data file in the Filename field, as shown in Figure 7-21.

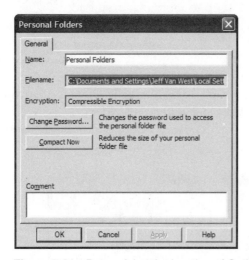

Figure 7-21   Determining the location of Outlook data files.

Once you know the location of the Outlook data file, you can include the entire folder that contains the data file in your list of folders to back up. For example:
`C:\Documents and Settings\<username>\Local Settings\Application Data\Microsoft\Outlook\`
The Local Settings folder is hidden by default and may not be available if you browse for the folder. You can still copy and paste the directory location into your backup software. You can also use the Folder Options control panel to show hidden files and folders.

Note   Close Outlook before backing up the Outlook data files.

Security Concerns

If your data contains privileged information, unscrupulous persons might use it in ways you do not want them to. Your tablet may have built-in security and encryption software and hardware that are beyond the scope of this book, but anyone can add password security from the Power Options control panel. If this is a concern for you, open the Power Options control panel to the Advanced tab and check the Prompt For Password When Computer Resumes From Standby check box as shown in Figure 7-22. Once this box is checked, the computer will be locked whenever it resumes from standby or hibernation, and the computer will require your login password to function. If you need this additional security, you may want to increase the duration before your computer automatically switches into standby so that you aren't constantly reentering your password.

Figure 7-22   Require that the user enter his or her password when the computer resumes from standby.

Hibernation: The Traveler's Friend

As you travel, you must start and stop your tablet several times; turn it on to prove to security personnel it really is a computer, turn it off while you board the airplane and while it climbs, turn it on to work, off while you watch the movie, on to find your hotel reservations, and so on. Hibernation is often the best option for these situations. Shutting the tablet down and restarting it takes a lot of time. Standby is a low-power mode, but it still draws power, and some applications can actually wake the computer from standby without your knowledge. Switching your tablet to standby also does not comply with the regulation to turn it off during takeoff and landing on an airplane. Hibernation allows for a relatively fast on and off, but draws no power and is considered turning the computer off as far as the FAA is concerned. If you have a second battery, hibernation is also a great way to change batteries without completely shutting down or plugging the tablet into a power outlet.

Tip   If your tablet has a laptop configuration, set it that way to get through airport security. Laptops are a familiar sight, and security personnel ask fewer questions.

Be Prepared to Share

One of the Tablet PC team members was working on his tablet on an airline flight and noticed that the person sitting next to him kept looking over. The Tablet PC team member smiled back and then noticed the other passenger was reading a Wall Street Journal article about the Tablet PC! As you travel with your new tablet, you may find yourself responding to a lot of people's curiosity. I spent twenty minutes each with a flight attendant and an airport security agent who had read about the tablet and wanted to know more.

E-Mail in Your Lap

Sitting in the airport waiting for your flight is a perfect time to sit and review your e-mail. Anticipating this, you already downloaded your messages before you left and switched Outlook to work offline as described earlier in the chapter. The other helpful trick for improving your Outlook experience on the tablet is customizing the Outlook layout and toolbars.

The Outlook layout was designed around a landscape orientation and doesn't work as well in the portrait mode when horizontal space is at a premium. Portrait mode is more comfortable on a tablet. The default Outlook layout uses the Outlook Bar. The Outlook Bar is handy, but its large icons use a lot of space, and there's no button to quickly show and hide it. Most of the Outlook Bar functions are available using the Folder List instead. In addition, the Advanced toolbar contains buttons to show and hide the Folder List with a single tap and has plenty of room for adding custom buttons for commonly used tablet commands, such as Work Offline. Figure 7-23 shows Outlook in a portrait orientation with the Outlook Bar and with the Folder List and the Advanced toolbar with custom buttons added.

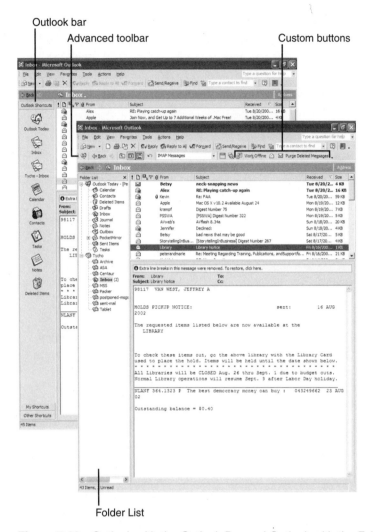

Figure 7-23   Outlook with the Outlook Bar and Outlook with the Folder
List and the Advanced toolbar.

To adjust your Outlook layout, open the Toolbars submenu on the View
menu and check the Advanced toolbar. Next use the View menu to uncheck the
Outlook Bar. Now you can use the Folder List button on the Advanced toolbar
to quickly show and hide the Folder List and maximize your limited horizontal
space. The Advanced toolbar also has a button for show/hide of the Preview
pane. Turning off the Preview pane lets you see all your e-mail subjects without
seeing the contents as you select them. This is handy if you are quickly deleting
many messages you are certain you no longer want.

To add custom buttons to the Outlook toolbars, tap the Customize option on the Tools menu. The Commands tab, shown in Figure 7-24, lists all the command categories on the left and the commands in that category on the right.

Figure 7-24   The Customize dialog box allows you to add custom buttons to the Outlook toolbars.

Find a command you use often, such as Work Offline, in the right-hand pane, and drag it up to the toolbar. If there was an icon next to the command, the icon will appear on the toolbar. If not, the text will appear on the toolbar as a button. You can also use the Customize feature to remove items from any toolbar.

> **Tip**   With Outlook on a tablet, the keyboard command you will miss the most is probably Delete. Don't forget about the Delete button on the Standard toolbar (it's a large X), and keep in mind the possibility of mapping Delete to a hardware button.

Journal on the Road

Part of my trip had me driving to a hotel and a seminar center in Ohio. As is often common now, the client sent me directions using an Internet mapping service, so my directions were on a Web page. To take the directions with me on my tablet, I could have made the Web page available offline. I wanted something a bit more versatile, however, so I imported the Web pages into Journal instead.

Since the Web page I wanted wasn't a document on my hard drive, I actually printed it into Journal to import it. To do this, select Print from the File menu in Internet Explorer. Next choose Journal Note Writer as the printer, as shown in Figure 7-25, and tap Print. A Save As dialog box will appear, allowing you to specify a location and a name for the new note. The new note will then open in Journal with the Web page as its background.

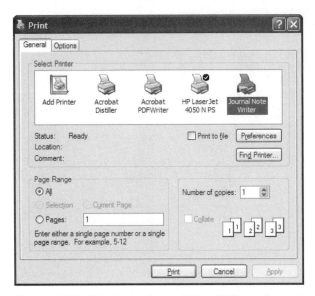

Figure 7-25   Printing to Journal Note Writer to import a document into Journal.

I actually wanted a few maps at different magnifications, so I printed it a few different ways. I also printed my airline, hotel, and car rental information, my client contact information, and the seminar schedule and combined all the pages into a single Journal note. This note now contained all of my trip information in the order in which I needed it. By setting the view to reading view, I could easily page through it one-handed, even while driving. Since it was a note, I could also highlight and make notes on the document as I traveled, such as adding the phone number shown in Figure 7-26 that I wrote down while waiting for a rental car in Columbus.

> **Tip**   The tablet screen can be difficult to read in outdoor sunlight. If you know you'll use a tablet document outside, make it as high contrast (bold black text on a white background) as possible. If you're driving, holding the tablet closer to the roof often cuts the glare and makes it easier to read.

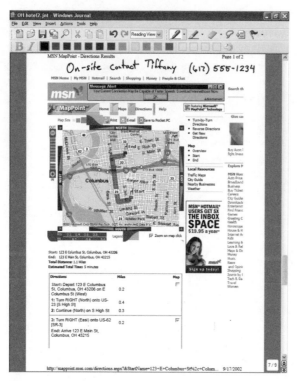

Figure 7-26 Build a travel document in Journal containing all of your important data.

Mapping Software on the Go

One of the members of the Tablet PC team installed mapping software on his tablet for a trip to New England. Wherever he went, he had maps from the state level to the street level at his fingertips. We agreed that a portable global positioning system (GPS) connected to the tablet that automatically updated his actual position on the map would have made it truly complete. Then again, what's the fun of vacation if you don't let yourself get a little lost once in a while?

Meetings and Collaborations

One of the great disadvantages of a conventional laptop in a meeting is the "clamshell" design. When you have the laptop open so that you can see the screen, the screen itself is a barrier between you and the person you're talking with. Furthermore, there's always room for wonder in their mind whether you're really listening or just playing Minesweeper. The tablet changes this phenomenon entirely. Not only is there no barrier, but also they can see what you are working on, and it's actually easy to hand them the tablet to look at as you discuss specific items. (Although if it is the first time they have seen a tablet, you might have to spend a few moments giving them a tour of its features.)

> **Tip**   Battery life is critical in meetings where you might be on batteries for a long time. Review the suggestions for extending battery life in Chapter 1 if you use your tablet this way.

Another great use for Journal is working collaboratively in a meeting while referencing a document. On this trip, I had to review some concepts in a PowerPoint presentation with two colleagues. I imported the PowerPoint presentation into Journal, and we passed around the tablet and wrote notes directly on the slides, as shown in Figure 7-27. I later converted these notes to text and added them to my slide show notes for my presentation.

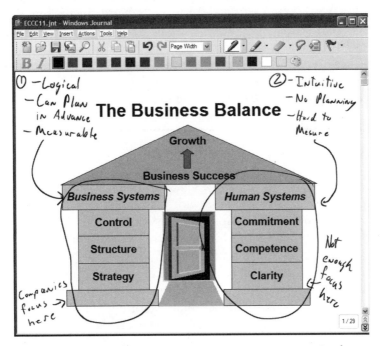

Figure 7-27   Journal is a great way to prepare your own notes for a presentation or a meeting.

Document Readers—Tablet Must-Have Apps

Document readers for PCs have been around for some time, but on the tablet they offer a whole new level of utility. Two free document readers you should install on your tablet are Adobe Acrobat Reader and Microsoft Reader. Acrobat Reader is a powerful and intuitive tool capable of presenting long, complex documents in a format easily read and navigated on the computer screen. If you purchase the full Acrobat application, it includes tools for bookmarking, indexing, zooming in and out, selecting and highlighting text, and filling out forms. Acrobat documents can even include JavaScript code and interact with Web sites. For this reason, Acrobat Portable Document Format (.pdf) files have become a standard for documentation and file transfer through much of the technical and print publication industry. Microsoft Reader is designed more for leisure and reference reading and features easy document navigation, bookmarks, and selection and highlighting tools. Microsoft Reader also uses Microsoft ClearType technology, which creates softer, more easily read type on laptops and LCD screens. With any of the thousands of book titles available, Microsoft Reader turns your tablet into an electronic book. Microsoft also has a free add-on for Word 2002 that will export your Word documents into the Reader eBook format.

Acrobat Reader is available at *http://www.adobe.com/products/acrobat/readstep2.html*. Adobe's Acrobat eBook Reader is also available on their Web site. Microsoft Reader and the Word 2002 add-on software are available at *http://www.microsoft.com/reader/*.

Making Presentations

Once you've mastered the cool presentation pen tools discussed in Chapter 6, making PowerPoint presentations with your tablet is essentially the same as making presentations with a laptop. One potential conflict, however, is that if you have your tablet set up without its keyboard available, you no longer have access to all the keyboard shortcuts shown in Figure 7-28. These shortcuts are very handy during a slide show. You can still access most of the commands on the slide show shortcut menu, but that distracts from your presentation. A better solution is to remap your hardware buttons for the appropriate commands, as described in Chapter 1. Since PowerPoint runs in landscape configuration, you can remap the buttons for the primary landscape orientation and leave the buttons you normally use in portrait orientation untouched. If your projector can flip an image upside down and project it, you can even use the secondary landscape orientation as a custom PowerPoint setup. Since I had only three buttons available, I mapped them to the three most important functions for me: next slide, previous slide, and a black screen.

> **Tip**   Be sure to switch your power scheme to one that does not let your tablet standby, hibernate, or turn off the screen automatically during your presentation.

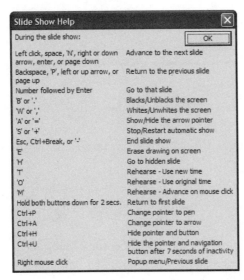

Figure 7-28   If you don't have a keyboard available while you present, change the hardware buttons for a landscape orientation to provide key PowerPoint commands.

> **Note**   For help troubleshooting problems with connecting your laptop to a video projector, see the section on "Using External Monitors" in Appendix A.

The Missing Link: A Bluetooth Video Connector

The *coup de grace* for interactivity in a presentation with a tablet would be a wireless video connection between the tablet and a video projector so that you could carry your tablet while you gave the presentation. Imagine navigating and annotating your slides while simultaneously moving about the room. Everything you did on the tablet screen would be mirrored on the projected screen without tying you down to one location. I'm not aware of any hardware that can do this yet, but given the possibilities, I hope it isn't far off.

Key Points

- Use offline files and offline Web pages to keep network files available as you travel.

- Use Outlook or your regular e-mail client in an offline mode when you work off the network.

- If you run into trouble with a wireless network, experiment with network settings for Wireless Equivalent Privacy (or WEP), type of key, and authentication.

- Create a traveling backup solution that accommodates all of your important data and allows instant access to individual files.

- Use the Folder List, Advanced toolbar, and custom toolbar buttons for a better Outlook experience in portrait orientation.

- Import maps, directions, and other key information into Journal for quick access as you travel.

- Map your hardware buttons in landscape orientation for important PowerPoint commands.

8

Additional Tablet Features

This chapter discusses a couple of additional features on the tablet that you might not be aware of. Sticky Notes is a tablet application that you can use to quickly jot down notes. Inkball is a pen-based game that is available only on the tablet. The end of this chapter has some thoughts on the future of the tablet.

Sticky Notes

Sticky Notes is a simple application for jotting down quick notes in ink and making short voice recordings. The main advantage to Sticky Notes is that it launches quickly, so there's no waiting for the program to open while trying not to forget the phone number you want to write down. While Sticky Notes is not nearly as sophisticated and versatile as Windows Journal, the ink you write on a sticky note can be copied over to Journal and Microsoft Office ink areas or converted into an Office picture.

Since I hardly ever convert my handwriting to text, I almost always use Sticky Notes [instead of Journal].
– Kamish Tumsi, Tablet PC team

> **Tip**   To take advantage of Sticky Notes' fast-launch ability, make sure you have the icon available on the Quick Launch bar on the Windows taskbar.

All of your sticky notes are kept in a single stack, which you can browse through with the Next Note and Previous Note buttons in the sticky note window or Page Up and Page Down keys on a standard keyboard. As shown in Figure 8-1, the sticky notes window also shows the date/time stamp for the note and how many notes you have total and provides buttons to create a new note, delete the current note, drag and drop the current note, copy the current note, and record and playback voice. To create a new sticky note, simply tap New Note and start writing. Each sticky note is one page only, so if you need more space you can either make the sticky notes window larger or continue writing on a second note. If you resize the window to create a large note and then later resize it smaller to take up less screen space, the large note will have scrollbars to get to any ink that is now hidden.

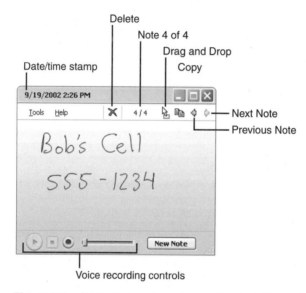

Figure 8-1   Sticky Notes allows for quick note taking in ink and short voice recordings.

Scratch Out Gesture

There's no eraser tool in Sticky Notes and no way to select individual ink strokes and remove them. Sticky Notes does, however, provide an optional scratch out gesture. It works similarly to the scratch out gesture in Journal in that it removes whatever ink strokes intersect the scratch out, rather than ink that is covered by the scratch out, and it requires a fast motion consisting of many horizontal strokes. If the scratch out gesture isn't working for you, make sure it is enabled by tapping the Tools menu, tapping Options, and adding a check mark next to Enable Scratch-out Gesture. Also, make sure your strokes are quick and strictly horizontal strokes, cutting through the middle of the ink you want erased. Even though there is no eraser tool, pens with an eraser will erase ink in Sticky Notes as a stroke eraser if you have that function enabled on the Tablet And Pen Settings control panel.

> **Caution**   Be careful what you scratch out or erase. There is no Undo in Sticky Notes.

Voice Recording

You can also put a quick voice memo on any sticky note in the stack. As with written sticky notes, voice notes are for recording short bits of information and ideas, rather than entering long speeches, and there is no text conversion ability. It's less important to have a good microphone with voice notes than with speech input on the input panel, but the better the microphone and the less ambient noise, the better your recording will be.

> **Tip**   The only indication that there is a voice recording on a sticky note is whether the play button is grayed out. Because that's pretty subtle, it's a good idea to put a short written note on the note saying there is a recording attached.

To record voice, choose an existing note or create a new one and tap the Record button. When you are done, tap the Stop button. If you want to add more to your recording, tap Record again, and the recorder will pick up where you left off. To listen to the voice on a note, tap the Play button. While the note is playing, the slider shows your place in the recording as it slides to the right. You can skip ahead or back in the recording by dragging the slider and pause the recording using the Pause button. If you delete the note, you delete the voice recording as well.

> **Caution**   If you pause the playback of a voice note and then start recording, the recording begins where you paused and writes over the original recording from that point forward.

Drag and Drop vs. Copy and Paste

While you can't select part of a sticky note, you can copy the entire thing. As with almost every other ink feature we've looked at, exactly how you do it determines the result. There are two ways to copy the contents of a sticky note. If you tap the Drag And Drop button, the entire note is selected with a solid outline, as shown in Figure 8-2, similar to when an ink area is selected as an object in Microsoft Word.

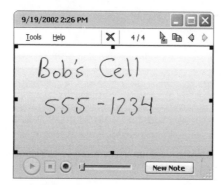

Figure 8-2   When you click the Drag And Drop button, the current note is selected.

If you drag the selected sticky note into an open Journal note, the actual ink strokes will be inserted into Journal, as shown in Figure 8-3.

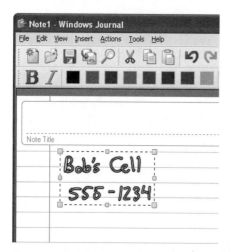

Figure 8-3   Ink from a sticky note dragged into a Journal note.

Dragging the body of a sticky note to any Office program inserts it as an Enhanced Windows Metafile (.emf) picture containing both the note content and the note background and date/time stamp, but it can still appear one of two ways. Figure 8-4 shows how the sticky note picture appears in Microsoft Excel, which is similar to how it appears in Microsoft PowerPoint.

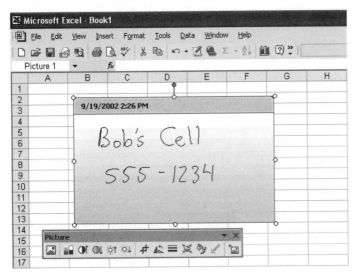

Figure 8-4   Ink from a sticky note dragged into Excel.

If you drag a sticky note into Microsoft Outlook or Word, the picture appears as an icon that you must double-tap to open and view. Figure 8-5 shows a sticky note dragged into an Outlook task.

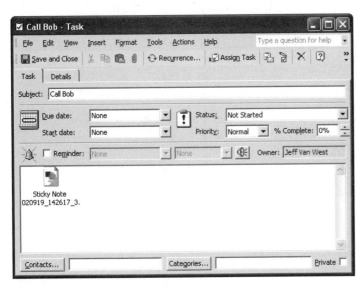

Figure 8-5   Ink from a sticky note dragged into an Outlook task.

If you want the actual picture of the sticky note to appear in your Word document or Outlook item, rather than the icon, tap the Copy button on the sticky note rather than the Drag And Drop button. Next tap in the Office document to place the cursor, select Paste Special from the Edit menu, and select Picture (Metafile), as shown in Figure 8-6.

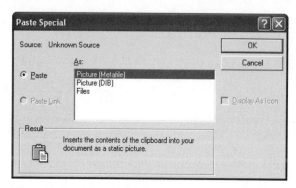

Figure 8-6   Using Paste Special to paste a sticky note.

After you tap OK, the picture contents are visible directly in the document, as shown in Figure 8-7.

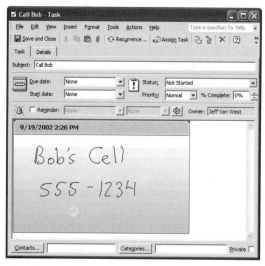

Figure 8-7   A sticky note pasted into an Outlook task using Paste Special.

> **Note**   While you can copy from a sticky note, there is no pasting anything into a sticky note.

Copy and Paste of Voice Notes

If you drag and drop a sticky note containing voice into another document, the voice recording is never included. If you copy and paste a sticky note containing voice into Outlook or Word using the normal Paste command, as opposed to Paste Special, two icons will appear in the document, as shown in Figure 8-8: one for the sticky note and the other for the audio. In this case, double-tapping the picture icon will open the picture and double-tapping the audio icon will play the voice recording.

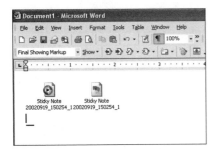

Figure 8-8   A sticky note containing voice pasted into an Outlook item or a Word document will have two icons: one for the sticky note and the other for the audio.

> **Tip**   A quick way to turn a sticky note into a stand-alone metafile picture and a .wav audio file (if the note contains audio) is to tap the Copy button and paste the note to the desktop or to a folder. Once the note is an .emf file and the audio is a .wav file, they can be inserted into the application of your choice.

Tools and Options

The Tools menu offers the option to export all of your notes into a single file as well as import a file containing one or several sticky notes. This file is readable only by Sticky Notes, so its main uses are letting another tablet user have a copy of your note file or backing up a large stack of notes. If you import a notes file into Sticky Notes, the two files are merged and new notes are added onto your existing notes. In the Import dialog box, there's an option to replace your existing notes with the imported file. If you choose this option, all of your existing notes are permanently deleted.

The Tools menu also controls the options for the scratch out gesture, deletion confirmation, and how Sticky Notes will launch and appear. If you use Sticky Notes often and for important information, you may want to adjust these settings so that Sticky Notes is always on top when maximized and confirms deletions before permanently removing the note.

> **Tip** To make drag and drop from Sticky Notes easier, turn on the Always On Top option temporarily and then turn it off when you are done.

Inkball

When you've had enough of working for a while and decide to play a game on your tablet, you'll find that, except for Pinball, all the games included with Windows XP work well with a pen. The tablet also comes with a brand new game that requires a pen and is only available to tablet users: Inkball.

Inkball is sort of a modern Pong or Breakout type of game in which you use ink strokes instead of a paddle. The goal is to bounce colored balls off ink strokes you lay down on the game board and put them in holes of the matching color without letting any balls enter holes of a different color. Once a stroke is hit by the ball, it disappears, so you will need pretty continuous pen work as the boards get more difficult. You're awarded points by how fast you clear the board and by the color of the balls you sink. Gray balls are worth nothing but can go in any hole, Red are worth 200, Blue 400, Green 800, and Gold 1600. Just to keep things interesting, there is also a time limit, walls that disappear or only block certain balls, walls that change the color of the balls, and ramps that speed up or slow down balls. As shown in Figure 8-9, the boards incorporate more and more elements as you move from beginner to expert. For examples and an explanation of all the different game elements, see the Inkball Help.

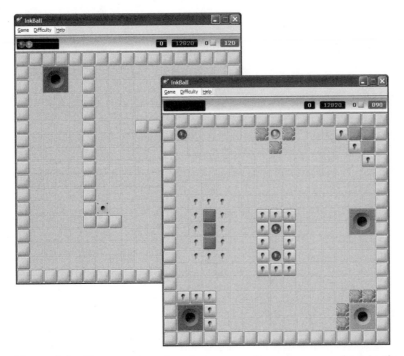

Figure 8-9 The game boards get more complex as you move from beginner to expert.

Drawing Ink Strokes

If there's a key to Inkball, it is understanding how a ball will bounce off the
ink and laying down those strokes well in advance of the ball. While the possibilities are nearly endless, here are four basic moves to get you going.

The Flat Shot

A flat shot just reverses the direction of the ball. In a pinch, just tapping a quick dot directly in front of the ball has the same effect. Figure 8-10 shows what this looks like.

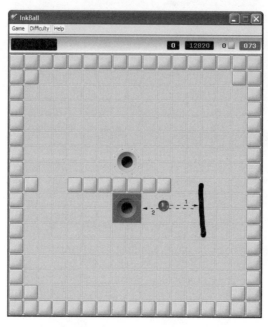

Figure 8-10   The flat shot in Inkball.

The Bumper Shot

Just like a bumper shot in billiards, the angle the ball hits a stroke determines the angle it leaves. Forty-five-degree bounces are the easiest to predict, but virtually any angle is possible. These shots work best if you have a moment to plan them out before the ball gets there. Figure 8-11 shows what this looks like.

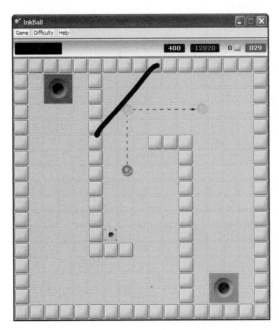

Figure 8-11   The bumper shot in Inkball.

The Curve Trap

Like a concave mirror, a curved stroke generally sends a ball back toward a specific point no matter what angle it arrived from. This shot is handy for convincing a stubborn ball to get into the hole. It helps to lay down two or three curves on top of one another, so if the first one doesn't do the job, the second or third will. See Figure 8-12.

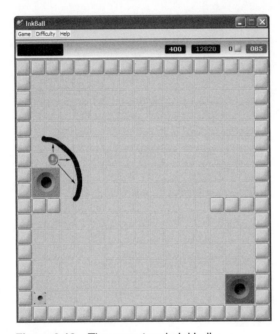

Figure 8-12   The curve trap in Inkball.

The Defensive Ring

One of the hardest parts of Inkball is trying to keep the balls you aren't working on out of trouble while you focus on getting a specific ball sunk. One way
to do it is to totally block off the holes you don't want balls to enter with lots
of separate circles. The circles can overlap, but they need to be many separate strokes so that it will take several collisions before the hole is exposed. A
variant on this technique is walling a ball into a corner with a bunch of flat or
curve strokes. See Figure 8-13.

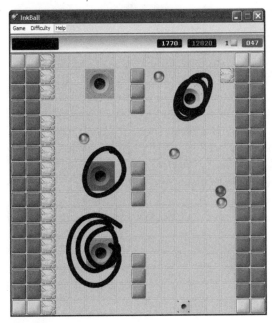

Figure 8-13   Defensive rings in Inkball.

Inkball Tips

Inkball is a great game, and you'll develop your own favorite techniques as
you play. Here are a few more tips to help as you learn the ropes:

- Spend some time on the beginner level to really learn how ink
  strokes affect the ball. These boards are sometimes so easy you
  can win without doing anything, but they are the best place to
  learn how to play.

- Watch the color of the balls queued up in the upper left before
  they come out and plan your first few ink strokes to send them in
  the right direction.

- Pause the game on the harder boards to figure out a strategy.

- You can draw ink over walls, so don't worry about making neat strokes on the game board.

- If you set up a trap with many ink strokes and don't use them all, use the Clear Ink command on the Game menu to get rid of them.

- When things get too fast, you can slow down a ball by creating a head-on collision with another ball. It's not easy, but it does work.

- Don't focus on one part of the board too long! Balls in other parts of the board have a way of getting into trouble if you don't keep an eye on them.

Tablet PC PowerToys

PowerToys are extra tools created by a development team that are not officially part of a product, but add cool functions or fun accessories. Keep an eye out on the Tablet PC Web site *http://www.microsoft.com/windowsxp/tabletpc/* for Tablet PC Power-Toys. Until then, you can take advantage of PowerToys for Windows XP at *http://www.microsoft.com/windowsxp/pro/downloads/powertoys.asp.*

Tablet PC—Today and Tomorrow

After living and working with a tablet for several months, I have decided my perfect personal information architecture is a digital data and mobility triangle like the one shown in Figure 8-14. At the top of the triangle and the center of my work would be my tablet. It would house my e-mail, all the files I was currently working on, and all the files I just like to have handy. I'd use it every day, take it with me most places I went, and do most of my work on it. At my desk, I would use it through an external monitor, mouse, and keyboard and the rest of the time use the pen. On one lower corner of the triangle would be my old networked desktop computer. Desktops are now relatively inexpensive to upgrade with faster processors and bigger storage drives. My desktop computer would keep an archive of all my files (including a synchronized copy of the My Documents folder on my tablet), burn my CDs, and be used for graphics or video work that required serious computational power and time. On the other corner of the triangle would be a cell phone with a calendar and a contacts list. The cell phone would synchronize with Outlook on the tablet so that I had that information available all the time. The tablet is very portable, but it still won't fit in your jacket pocket. These three interconnected information systems would provide a range of power and portability to match any situation.

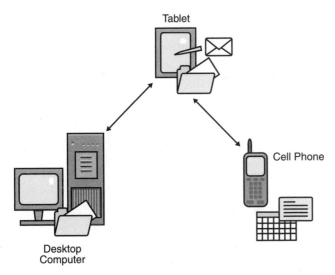

Figure 8-14   A possible personal information architecture based on the tablet.

Of course, that's just my ideal using technology available today. While working with the Tablet PC team at Microsoft, I was given a few glimpses into the next version of the Tablet PC Edition of Windows and had a chance to see some of the cool tablet hardware still in development. As the Tablet PC Edition of Windows matures and hardware improves, the tablet will deliver more and more thoroughly on the promise of being your one computer that you use in more places than ever before. What I saw was only a small piece of the future, but I assure you the future looks bright.

Key Points

- Use Sticky Notes for jotting down quick notes that don't need to be converted to text.

- The Sticky Notes application does not have an eraser tool, but you can use the scratch out gesture to delete ink strokes, or you can just delete the entire note.

- You can add short voice recording to sticky notes.

- If you drag and drop a sticky note into Journal, the ink strokes are maintained. If you drag and drop a sticky note into an Office application, the note is converted to a picture.

- Use Paste Special to get a sticky note picture to appear in a Word document or an Outlook item.

- Experiment with the various Inkball shots, using the beginner boards to really understand how the balls react to ink.

- Stay tuned to the world of pen computing. Everything described in this book is just the beginning!

Part IV

Appendixes

A

Troubleshooting

Ideally, this book has given you enough information to perform your own basic troubleshooting on your tablet. If you can't figure out the problem fairly quickly, the next best step is the Help and Support system, shown in Figure A-1, available through the Help And Support option on the Start menu.

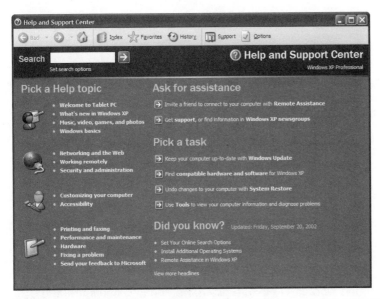

Figure A-1 The Help and Support system of Windows XP is interactive and helps you isolate the problem.

This interactive Help is far more capable than previous Windows Help systems and is linked to several built-in diagnostic tools, troubleshooting wizards, thousands of individual topics, and the online database known as the

Microsoft Knowledge Base. The Knowledge Base contains thousands of articles containing step-by-step explanations of common fixes and useful tips, such as the one shown in Figure A-2. Because the Knowledge Base is on the Web, you should connect to the Internet to get full utility out of Windows XP Help and Support.

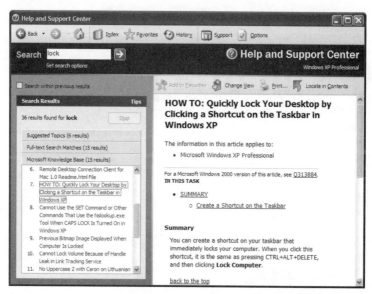

Figure A-2   Help and Support is linked to the Knowledge Base Web site.

Most of the problems you encounter will not be issues specific to the Tablet PC Edition of Windows XP, but here are some strategies to help troubleshoot the most common snags that are specific to the tablet or are likely to be encountered by tablet users.

> **Tip**   Windows XP has built-in features that allow another Windows user to connect to your computer remotely and administer it. These features are named Remote Assistance and Remote Desktop. If you will be on the road often and have good IT support staff or a knowledgeable friend who can help in a pinch, get them to configure and test these features in person before you need help from some far-off location.

Pen and Digitizer Problems

If the pen is not behaving correctly, the problem could be in the hardware of the pen itself or the software that interprets the signals. If the pen is working very poorly or not at all, try attaching a USB mouse to control the tablet while you troubleshoot.

First check out the hardware.

■ Try another pen if one is available. The pen is the most likely failure if you are having a hardware problem. If you don't have a backup pen already, you should seriously consider getting one.

■ If your pen uses batteries, make sure the batteries are installed and working.

■ If your tablet is running on batteries, plug it in. It's unlikely that low power is the culprit because the power draw for the pen and digitizer is far less than for the screen, but it's best to eliminate the possibility.

■ Make sure you're holding the pen fairly upright and pressing down firmly on the screen to write or tap. The tip of the pen must actually compress slightly to register contact with the screen.

■ Check that none of the pen buttons are stuck in the pressed position. You should be able to feel each button press down and come back up. Use the Tablet And Pen Settings control panel to disable the press and hold, barrel button, and top of pen eraser. If this fixes the problem, you have a stuck button. By turning these functions back on one at a time, you can figure out which button it is. If press and hold is the problem, then that button is the one that is compressed when you press down with the tip of the pen on the screen.

Next try the software.

■ Recalibrate the screen for the appropriate mode, landscape or portrait. If your pen works well in one screen orientation but not the other, calibration is a likely culprit.

■ If the pen does not work at all but an external mouse or trackpad does, try restarting the tablet with no external USB or FireWire items attached and see whether the pen works then.

■ If the pen stopped working after installing new software or devices, you might have a corrupted file or driver conflict. This is unlikely, but it is possible. Windows XP provides a utility to restore the system to an earlier point, and it creates these system restore points every time you install software, patches, or drivers compatible with this feature. System restore does not affect any of your data files, so your work will be left unharmed; however, it's a good idea to back up all your data before doing anything to your system. If the pen works after a system restore, that was the problem. If not, you might want to undo the restore because it wasn't the problem and could interfere with the last program or device you installed.

- If the pen still isn't working, you should contact your hardware manufacturer for further troubleshooting.

System Restore

To perform a system restore, close all open applications and then choose Help And Support from the Start menu. Under Pick A Task, select Undo Changes To Your Computer With System Restore. When the System Restore screen appears, as shown in Figure A-3, select the Restore My Computer To An Earlier Time option.

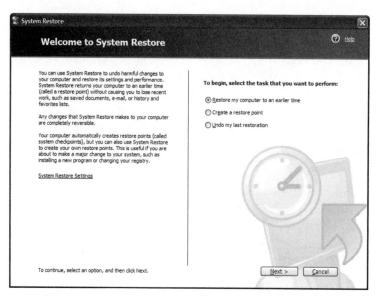

Figure A-3   Use System Restore to return your tablet to an earlier working state.

> **Note**   The Undo My Last Restoration option for System Restore appears only after you have restored the system to an earlier configuration.

Select the restore point you want using the calendar and the description of the last restore point, as shown in Figure A-4. If you installed multiple software packages on one day, there may be many restore points. Select a date prior to the pen and digitizer problem.

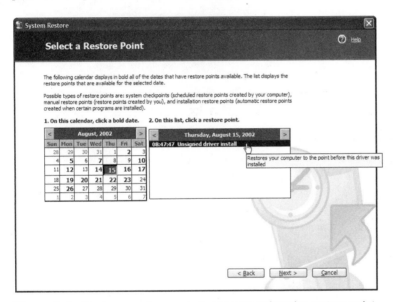

Figure A-4   During a system restore, you can select the restore point.

After you select a restore point, the confirmation screen appears as shown in Figure A-5.

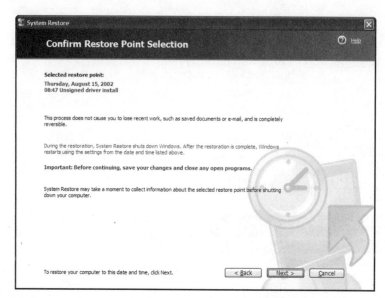

Figure A-5 The confirmation screen during a system restore.

After you tap Next, Windows will shut down, restore the system, and restart. When you log back in, the system will be back to its earlier point.

Network Problems

Troubleshooting network problems could be a book chapter all by itself, but overall the key is isolating the problem. The Help And Support Network Troubleshooter will walk you through a process to do exactly that, but here is an overview of the steps involved.

- Is your tablet actually connecting to the network? Before any network service can work properly, the tablet must communicate with the network. To view the status of your current network connection, open the Network Connections control panel. Network Connections will list your current high-speed and modem connections, as shown in Figure A-6.

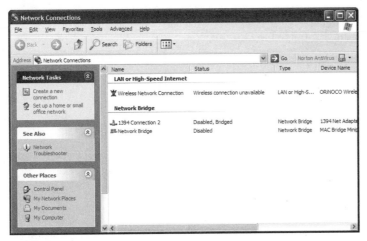

Figure A-6 The Network Connections control panel shows the status of your network connections.

Network connections that are not working will have a red X through them. If you see the red X, then that is your problem. If you're trying to connect to a wireless network, right-tap the wireless connection icon, select Properties, and tap the Wireless Networks tab to list all the available networks. If none are available, you are out of range, the network is closed to outside access and requires a custom connection, or your network hardware is not working. In this situation, try a different network connection, such as a wired connection instead of a wireless one.

Tip   If you've enabled the option, you can see the connection status of any network in the notification area of the Windows taskbar. You can enable this option in the Properties dialog box for a network connection. Right-tap a network connection in the Network Connections control panel, and select Properties from the shortcut menu. On the General tab, make sure Show Icon In Notification Area When Connected is checked as shown in Figure A-7. You must check this option for each wired, wireless, and modem connection you create. This is very handy if you hop on and off networks often.

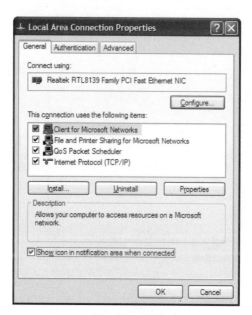

Figure A-7 Enabling the option to view network connection status in the notification area of the Windows taskbar.

- If the network is connected, is the problem with the entire network or a network service? For example, if Internet Explorer isn't working, but you can log in to a file server, the file sharing services are working but Internet services are not. If no services are working, make sure you have the correct type of login for the network, workgroup vs. domain login, and a valid user name and password. See Chapter 7 for more information on logging on to various networks. You can also try selecting the network connection in the Network Connections control panel and tapping the Repair This Connection option in the list on the left-hand side of the window. Usually this option works only if you lost a network by taking the tablet out of range, and it's having trouble reconnecting when you come back in range.

- If only one service is not working, that service is probably not configured correctly for this network. This situation often requires the help of an IT person who knows that network. As a quick fix, you can try closing all the connections using that service, such as all your browser windows and your e-mail program, and then relaunching them. Another thing to try is switching to a different network connection, such as a wired connection instead of a wireless, and then switching back. Sometimes this will reestablish a broken service. It's also possible that your tablet is not the problem and that service is down on that network.

One annoying network problem that is particular to wireless networks is incompatible authentication. The symptom is that you can connect to a wireless network without problems, it suddenly disconnects after a few minutes, and then is immediately available for reconnection. Right-tap the wireless network connection in the Network Connections control panel, select Properties, tap the Wireless Network tab, select the wireless network you are having trouble with in the Preferred Networks area, and tap Properties. The properties on the Association tab are correct, otherwise you couldn't connect at all. Tap the Authentication tab and change the Enable IEEE 802.1x Authentication For This Network option as shown in Figure A-8

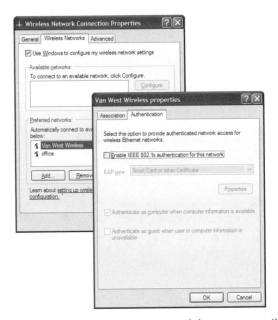

Figure A-8   If a wireless network keeps connecting, kicking you off, and then inviting you back on, try changing the network authentication option.

USB and FireWire Dos and Don'ts

If you're new to USB and FireWire, you'll find these devices much easier to work with than old serial and parallel peripherals. For the most part, you simply plug them in, wait a moment for them to be recognized, and then proceed. Both USB and FireWire are quite reliable under Windows XP and usually work flawlessly, but here are a couple of quick tips to help with problems if they do appear.

- USB and FireWire devices still require drivers to operate correctly. Many of these drivers ship with Windows XP, so you may be able to plug in the device and let Windows install the driver itself. If you have an install program that came with the device, it's usually better to run the installer before hooking up the device so that Windows makes the best choice for a driver.

- When you first connect and power up the device, the Add Hardware Wizard will launch and guide you through the setup process. On subsequent connections you may simply see a notification that the new hardware was found and configured for you, as shown in Figure A-9.

Figure A-9   Notification that new hardware is available for use.

- If the device isn't found automatically after a few seconds, try turning it off, unplugging it, plugging it back in, and powering it up again. If recognition continues to be a problem, restart the tablet with the device unplugged, and then connect it and turn it on. Getting the device recognized for the first time is the most common problem with USB and FireWire.

- When you want to disconnect the device be sure to stop it. Tap on the icon in the notification area for USB and FireWire peripherals and select the device you want to remove, as shown in Figure A-10.

Figure A-10   Stopping a device.

Depending on the device, you might see a dialog box asking you to verify the item you want stopped. If it appears, tap Stop, and then OK on the next screen. It's more likely, though, that the system will stop them automatically and display the notification that they can be removed, as shown in Figure A-11. Once the device is removed, you will need to turn it off and then back on or unplug and then plug it back in to use it again.

Figure A-11   Notification that a device can be removed.

Using External Monitors

While many laptops support multiple monitors, the idea of sometimes using a standard keyboard and an external monitor is practically fundamental to the tablet. Unlike large computer monitors where you can use one of many screen resolutions, the LCD screens found on tablets work best at only one screen resolution. LCD screens also have a slow refresh rate, which is the speed at which the image on the screen is redrawn. Slow refresh rates don't matter on an LCD screen, but on a normal monitor they cause a slight flicker that can give you a serious headache. If you attach your tablet to an external monitor and don't like what you see, try changing the screen resolution. To change the screen resolution, open the Display control panel, go to the Settings tab, and adjust the slider for screen resolution to a larger number. To increase the refresh rate, tap the Advanced button and then tap the Monitor tab. The available refresh rates appear in the list, as shown in Figure A-12. Usually the best results are achieved by selecting the highest setting available. Screen resolution and monitor refresh rate are interdependent. The larger your screen resolution, the slower the monitor may be able to refresh, so you might have to experiment to find the best balance.

> **Caution**   Do not uncheck the Hide Modes That This Monitor Cannot Display option. Doing so can allow you to select options that prevent you from seeing anything on the screen. If this does happen, just wait. The original settings should return after fifteen seconds.

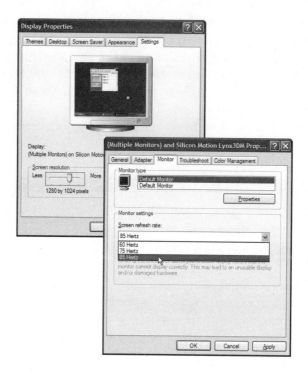

Figure A-12 Changing the refresh rate.

Mirrored Monitors vs. Extended Desktop

Some tablet hardware allows you to use different resolutions and refresh rates for the external monitor and the tablet screen. In this case, the two screens can act as one large extended desktop, and you can move your mouse and drag windows from one monitor to the other. The advanced settings should provide an option for which screen is primary and contains your taskbar, and which is secondary. You may even be allowed to keep the tablet in portrait mode with the external monitor in landscape mode. Other tablet hardware presents the same desktop on both the tablet screen and the external monitor, so you must switch the tablet to landscape orientation to use the external monitor. In some mirrored configurations, you must turn off the tablet screen to get a good refresh rate and resolution on the external monitor. Check your hardware owners manual for a way to turn off the tablet screen if you are having trouble getting a good picture on the external monitor.

If you have an extended desktop system, you must set up PowerPoint to use the correct screen for its slide show. In PowerPoint, select Set Up Show on the Slide Show menu to find the setting for multiple monitors.

B

Tablet Shortcuts

Pen Shortcuts

- **Press and hold and right-tap**   Use either or both functions to provide a right-click when you use your pen instead of a mouse. The exact behaviors of these functions are set in the Tablet And Pen Settings control panel.

- **Top of pen erase**   Where available, this shortcut allows you to erase ink without switching tools in Journal and Sticky Notes by pressing and dragging with the top of the pen instead of the point. Some pens also have a barrel button for an eraser. This function must be enabled in the Tablet And Pen Settings control panel.

- **Double-tap Input Panel title bar**   This toggles the input panel between docked and undocked.

- **Tap to select**   In Journal and an ink area, tapping an ink stroke with the Selection Tool will select the entire stroke.

- **Right-drag selection**   In Journal, holding down the pen barrel button while you drag a circle around ink will select that ink and then open the shortcut menu regardless of the tool you have selected.

Keystroke Shortcuts

- **Windows security key**   All tablets have this button to enter the Ctrl+Alt+Del keystroke when a standard keyboard is not attached. Use this button for login and logout as well as opening Task Manager to end non-responding programs.

- **Hardware buttons**   Some tablets have hardware buttons to which you can assign many useful commands and keystrokes. These associations are set in the Tablet And Pen Settings control panel. Some hardware will also have buttons permanently assigned to sleep or hibernate, control of external monitors, turning the wireless network card on and off, or other useful features.

Navigation Shortcuts

- **Tap or right-tap the Change Tablet And Pen Settings icon in the notification area**   Tapping the Change Tablet And Pen Settings icon opens a shortcut menu, allowing you to toggle the screen or sound on and off and change the screen orientation. The shortcut menu also contains an option to open the Tablet And Pen Settings control panel.

- **Pressing the Function hardware button twice**   If your tablet has a Function hardware button, pressing the Function button twice opens the Change Tablet And Pen Settings shortcut menu.

- **Tap the Battery/Power icon in the notification area**   Tapping the Battery/Power icon opens a shortcut menu of all your custom power schemes to allow quick switching. Double-tapping the icon opens the Power Meter dialog box, which shows the battery charge level. Right-tapping displays a shortcut menu, which includes an option to open the Power Options control panel.

- **Custom buttons**   While not tablet-specific shortcuts, on-screen buttons are even more useful on the tablet. Adding common items to your Quick Launch bar and Start menu and customizing your Office toolbars are very helpful.

Control Shortcuts

- **Print to Journal Note Writer**   Some screen items, such as Web pages, do not import easily into Journal. To import these items, print them to the Journal Note Writer printer.

- **Copy and paste a sticky note containing audio to the desktop**   This is the best way to create a .emf file of the note and a .wav file of the audio and use them outside Sticky Notes.

- **Paste ink into an Office application without an ink area**   Pasting ink into any Office application without opening an ink area first converts it to a picture. This provides many more format options at the expense of editability.

C

If You're New to Windows XP

Windows XP is a fully rebuilt version of Windows that makes use of the success of Windows 2000 and adds many unseen enhancements in stability, performance, and security. Windows XP comes in two versions, Windows XP Home Edition and Windows XP Professional. Your tablet runs Windows XP Tablet PC Edition, which is actually a version of Windows XP Professional with additional functionalities added.

New Features in Windows XP

Some of the differences you will see in Windows XP are:

- **New login screen and user accounts** Unlike Windows 95, Windows 98, and Windows Me, you must have a login account with a username and a password to use Windows XP. If security is not an issue for you, the tablet can log in to your account automatically at startup, but it's important to understand that the account is still there. Your desktop preferences (see Chapter 1), speech input profile (see Chapter 2), and My Documents and Favorites folders are all linked to a specific account. The login screen can be a dialog box requiring a typed name and password familiar to Windows NT and Windows 2000 users or a new Welcome screen where users choose their name from a list and then enter a password. The tablet automatically displays an on-screen keyboard to assist with login. Control of how users log in is set in the User Accounts control panel. The new Welcome screen is available only for computers that are not part of a domain.

> **Note**   If you need maximum security, use the classic Windows login rather than the Welcome screen. There is actually a small security risk because of the on-screen keyboard that could allow a skilled user to bypass the login screen. Requiring users to press the tablet security button eliminates this risk.

- **New visuals**   Windows XP introduces many new colors and special visual effects to enhance your desktop environment. Chapter 1 discusses some of these features and how they might impact performance on your tablet.

- **New Start menu**   The Start menu is organized into two columns with commonly used programs and locations updated dynamically. Ways to customize this menu are discussed in Chapter 1.

- **New folder windows**   Windows XP has several new options for viewing content. When you open a folder in Windows XP, by default there is a left pane that contains context-sensitive options, links to other folders and services, and details about the currently selected item. Each subpane is expandable or collapsible for easier viewing.

- **New Help and Support center**   As mentioned in Appendix A, Windows XP has a new Help and Support system that offers step-by-step troubleshooting and is linked to Microsoft's online Knowledge Base.

- **System restore**   Windows XP automatically maintains a database of earlier installations of your operating system and allows you to return the system to an earlier state if it is damaged or corrupted by installation of new software or hardware. See Appendix A for details.

- **New versions of Internet Explorer and Windows Media Player** Internet Explorer 6 includes new privacy settings. Windows Media Player 8 includes improvements at managing your music and video collection.

There are a lot of books on Windows XP Professional available for further information. Any good text on Windows XP Professional will apply to the Tablet PC Edition. One good book to check out is *Microsoft Windows XP Inside Out* (Microsoft Press, 2001).

Importing Data from Another PC

If you want to import your files and settings from your current computer running Windows to your new tablet, the File And Settings Transfer Wizard of Windows XP will guide you through the steps of bringing the information from one computer to the other. The wizard works with versions of Windows all the way back to Windows 95. All you need to get going is some way to move the data between the computers and your Windows XP installation CD. If at all possible, create a network connection between the two computers. If this isn't possible, use a removable drive such as a USB or FireWire drive discussed in Chapter 7 or a writable CD drive. It is possible to make a direct connection between the old and new computers using a serial cable, but avoid this direct connection option, unless you want to spend all day transferring files.

> **More Info**   For more detailed information about the File Settings And Transfer Wizard see Chapter 2 of *Microsoft Windows XP Inside Out.*

To use the Files And Settings Transfer Wizard, follow these steps:

1. Start the transfer process on the tablet by opening the File And Settings Transfer Wizard. On the Start menu, tap All Programs, Accessories, System Tools, and then Files And Settings Transfer Wizard. On the Welcome page, tap Next. On the subsequent page, set the tablet as the New Computer and tap Next.

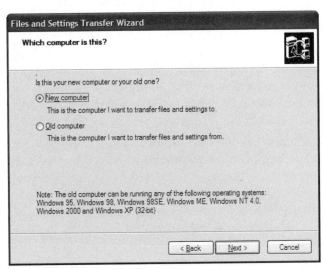

2. On the next page, choose I Will Use The Wizard From The Windows XP CD option and tap Next.

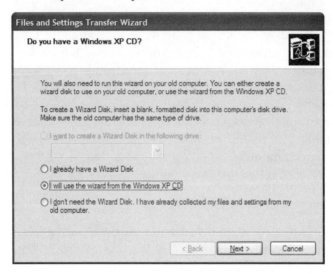

3. The next page tells you to run the wizard on your old computer. If your old computer is running Windows XP, you can run the Files And Settings Transfer Wizard on that computer and select the option for Old Computer. If it is running an earlier version of Windows, insert the Windows XP CD and select Perform Additional Tasks from the Welcome menù. Click Transfer Files And Settings to start the Files And Settings Transfer Wizard.

4. On the page asking for a transfer method, click Home Or Small Office Network if you're using the network or Other for removable drives and click Next. If the wizard is unable to find the new Windows XP computer, this option will be unavailable. This could be because the wizard isn't running on the new computer or the computers aren't on the same subnet, as described in the Knowledge Base article "'Home or Small Network' Option is Unavailable in the Files and Settings Transfer Wizard." See the article for more information.

5. The next page lets you determine exactly what you want transferred: settings, files, or both. Your settings not only include your desktop layout and settings but also include personal settings for virtually every program on your old computer, as well as items you might think of as files, such as e-mail messages in Outlook Express. Your files are exactly what you think, the files you work with on your computer. Unfortunately, the wizard transfers practically all of them, which can add up to gigabytes of data, unless you tell it otherwise. (See step 6.) The settings and files option transfers both.

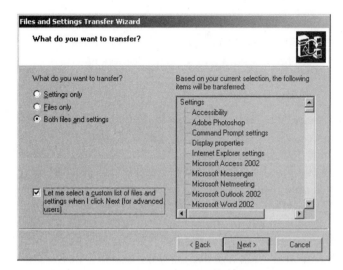

6.   If your tablet has at least as big a hard drive as your old computer *and* the two are networked, you can leave the option for selecting a custom list of files and settings unchecked. When you click Next on the old computer, the process will begin and could take more than 30 minutes. If you want to limit the files included, check the box for selecting a custom list, click Next, and complete these three steps:

❑   Select any setting you do not want transferred by selecting them in the list and tapping Remove. For example, the tablet uses very different display settings than a standard monitor, so these are best left behind. If you're not sure about whether or not to copy a setting, remove it from the list. You can always set it up fresh on your tablet.

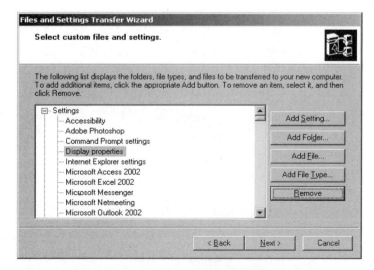

❑   Select the folders you want transferred. Commonly used folders, such as My Documents, appear in the list by default. You
may remove and add as many folders as you wish, even folders
on different drives, but every file and subfolder in the folder
will be transferred.

❑   Select the file types you do not want transferred and remove
them. This is a confusing option, because it does not affect the
folders you have selected for transfer in the previous step. In
other words, you could remove every file type from this list and
all the files in your selected folders and all your selected settings
would still transfer. In fact, if you are certain all the data you want
is contained in the folders you select, go ahead and remove
every file type from this list. It will speed up the transfer process.
If you are concerned there may be stray files, such as Word documents, that will be left behind, remove everything except those
file types from the list. The wizard will search every local drive
and folder on your old computer for these files and copy them.

7.   Begin the transfer from the old computer, and then go get a fresh
cup of coffee. If the computers are networked, the tablet will automatically start receiving the files, and each computer will tell you
when it is done. The tablet will be busy for quite a while after the old
computer is finished. Be patient. If you are using a removable drive,
when the old computer is finished you can remove the drive, connect it to the tablet, and tap Next on the tablet's wizard page. Locate
the files from the old computer on the removable drive, and tap
Next. The second cup of coffee while waiting for the files to install
onto your tablet is strictly optional.

Once you have your new system up and running, be sure to:

■   Write down your password, and save it in a safe place. Also, register
any smart cards or encryption keys if you plan to use them.

■   Set a system restore point using the System Restore utility.

■   Create a backup of your data and a schedule for regular backups in
the future. This might be a good use for your old computer.

Index

Symbols
@ character, entering with Input Panel, 35

A
accessing files offline
  e-mail messages, 200–205
    folders for, 200–203
    remote mail (reviewing before download), 204–205
  files and folders, 192–197
  Web pages, 197–199
account management, 208–212
  .NET Passport, 210
  network passwords and automatic login, 211
  Windows XP, 261
Acrobat Reader (Adobe), 224
adding pages to Windows Journal, 92–94
Adobe Acrobat Reader, 224
Advanced tab (Power Options control panel), 16
Alarms tab (Power Options control panel), 16
alternate words list (writing panel), 46
  effect on searching notes, 143, 145
annotation in Windows Journal, 135–136
arranging text boxes and pictures, 117
authentication with wireless networks, 208, 253
autohiding Input Panel, 74
autohiding the taskbar, 21
automatic file recovery, Windows Journal, 103–104
automatic wireless zero configuration, 206

B
background images, Journal pages, 119
  built-in templates, 121
  custom templates, 123–128, 131–133
  TIFF and Metafile backgrounds, 128–131
Backspace key, gesture for, 52
backup strategies, 213–216
  Outlook data backups, 216
  portable backup devices, 213–214
  software solutions, 214–215
ball game (InkBall), 234–240
batteries
  alarms at critical levels, 16
  during meetings and presentations, 223, 225
  pen use and, 11
  power management, 14–17
  recharging, 17
  switching, 16, 217
  tapping the Battery/Power icon, 258
bold, applying to ink, 109
brightness, screen, 26
browsing sticky notes, 228

built-in templates, Windows Journal, 121–123
bumper shot (InkBall stroke), 237
buttons. *See* hardware buttons

C
calibrating paper size, Windows Journal, 87
calibrating pen, 25–26
capitalization, recognizing, 46
cell phone backups, 214
Change Shape To commands, 113–114
character recognizer, 75
chisel pen (Windows Journal), 82
circles, drawing neatly, 113–114
ClearType technology, 140
clicking and dragging, how to, 10
collaboration with Windows Journal, 147–148
  advice for travelers, 222–223
color, page rules, 118
color of pen, setting, 74, 111–112
comments, inking into Word documents, 168–169
computers, transferring data to tablet, 263–267
configuring
  custom colors, 112
  hardware buttons, 8, 26–28
  importing settings from PC to tablet, 263–267
  offline file access, 192–193
  pen operation, 28–31
  pen width and color, 74, 109–112
    Tablet Pack ink area, 156
  power options, 14–17
  tablet settings, 25–28
  templates for Journal pages, 123–128, 131–133
  workspace appearance and features, 18–25
connection, network, 250. *See also* networking
control shortcuts, list of, 258
Convert Selection To command (Windows Journal), 184–187
converting handwriting to text. *See* handwriting recognition
copying ink
  into Office documents, 160–163
  sticky notes, 230–233
  Windows Journal, 100–101
    Outlook meeting information into, 187
    from Tablet Pack ink area, 162
correcting errors
  handwriting. *See* handwriting recognition
  speech recognition. *See* speech input
  voice commands for, 67
  Windows Journal text conversion, 101
crescent-shaped selections (Windows Journal), 97

Jeff Van West

Jeff Van West has more than nine years of experience as a freelance writer, corporate trainer, and instructional designer. He has worked internationally to facilitate collaborative projects in numerous fields, including information technology and the aviation industry. His books and multimedia technical training programs have been used in North America, Europe, Japan, and Australia. Jeff has also worked with using narrative as a teaching and unifying tool across functions in a variety of settings. Jeff lives with his wife and son in Seattle, Washington.

The manuscript for this book was prepared and galleyed using Microsoft Word. Pages were composed by Microsoft Press using Adobe FrameMaker+SGML for Windows, with text in Garamond and display type in Helvetica Condensed. Composed pages were delivered to the printer as electronic prepress files.

Cover Designer:	Patricia Bradbury
Cover Illustrator:	Todd Daman
Interior Graphic Designer:	James D. Kramer
Principal Compositors:	Dan Latimer, Kerri DeVault
Interior Artist:	Joel Panchot
Principal Copyeditor:	Patricia Masserman
Proofreader:	nSight, Inc.
Indexer:	Seth Maislin